The Power of Pure Stewardship

THE POWER OF PURE STEWARDSHIP

CARL W. BERNER SR.

CONCORDIA PUBLISHING HOUSE

SAINT LOUIS   LONDON

Concordia Publishing House, St. Louis, Missouri
Concordia Publishing House Ltd., London, E. C. 1
Copyright © 1970 Concordia Publishing House

Library of Congress Catalog Card No. 77-126536

MANUFACTURED IN THE UNITED STATES OF AMERICA

Contents

Foreword

In the title of this book the author signals the reader that we have a choice about something very important in life.

On the one hand, says the author, in effect, the church and its members can devise practices in stewardship that rely largely on earthbound patterns of thinking. These can be a combination of gimmicks and doodads that may be sincerely conceived but that inevitably fall of their own weight.

On the other hand, points out the author, one can rely on heavenly patterns that Christ set out so clearly and invitingly in the Gospel. Luther has called this choice a "leap of faith." This plunge lands the daring in an atmosphere where the spirit of man can soar. Why be ambivalent about the choice, the author asks. In a nutshell, he says in this book that the power lies in the pure.

Quite appropriately, the author narrates portions of his own life in the book's introductory pages. As he says in this portion, he had a choice to make, too—and he did it early in his ministry. He chose the power of the pure. Using this autobiographical sketch as a witness and a springboard for the book, the author then sets out the concepts of stewardship that resolutely avoid human engineering in favor of Biblically built-in blueprints that are easy to follow and deeply satisfying to the heart and soul.

The writer of this foreword was exposed to the sincerity and exuberance of Dr. Berner's teaching and preaching in stewardship for a number of years and gained greatly from the experience. So did thousands of others who had the good fortune to come under this pastor's influence during his long, faithful, and successful ministry. He started his work with a handful of parishioners, a financial shoestring, and a prayer. Under God's blessing, two congregations mushroomed and grew steadily in Christian maturity. What's more, the pastor importantly influenced hundreds of others who moved into and out of the geographical area he served.

Many pastors and laymen in many places have unquestionably done God-pleasing things in the use of time, talents, and possessions—and are still doing them. Be this as it may, Mickey Mouse in stewardship is much more evident than it ought to be.

This thoughtful book by Dr. Berner invites us all to reexamine and reassess. One can predict that the reader will not only enjoy this invitation to rethink his position but that he may very possibly see spiritual horizons in stewardship that are substantially wider and more colorful than he might have perceived before.

T. H. HARTMAN
Appleton, Wis.

Preface

The aim of this book is to present convincing proof that pure stewardship has power, while the polluted brand is weak and ineffective. As an aroused nation is, at this time, demanding the cleansing and safeguarding of our natural environment, so an alerted and concerned church would do well to set its mind upon restoring fresh and clean air to the contaminated stewardship climate.

I don't quite know whether to apologize or not for using the perpendicular pronoun so frequently in the first chapter. I don't even remotely regard my experience in stewardship as any kind of personal triumph. In fact, it isn't my story at all. I'm merely recording what was written by Another. Nothing in the story was devised or sought; it was all granted and wrought. Looking back, I can see clearly that it was all a blessing from on high.

Although it might have been desirable for me to preserve a stance of disinterest, I feel sure the reader will notice my earnest desire to influence others to follow the path on which God led me. Through many years of pastoral counseling I have learned that no one will ever do anything simply because someone else—even a pastor—says it. A person responds only because he is convinced that it is the right thing to do. I'm sure it will be abundantly clear that what I desire above all is that others experience, as I have, the mystery, miracle, and power that go with pure stewardship.

I would be untrue to what I feel in my heart if I failed to cite for well-deserved recognition the valiant service of the hundreds of members of Faith Church, who had a greater share in this book than they may realize. To all these, my good and faithful friends, I wish to say, "Thank you for your share in this story. You were the ones who wrote it as much or even more than I did."

In a very special way I desire to acknowledge my debt to Kirk L. Page, T. H. Hartman, Rev. Michael Keene, Dr. Kenneth L. Ahl, Edith Dibble, and my brother, Dr. Robert E. Berner, for their helpful guidance.

CARL W. BERNER
Inglewood, Calif.

1

The Story of a Christian Steward And How He Got That Way

From Perspiration to Pulpit

In the spring of 1925 I was one of the 88 graduates who assembled in the chapel of Concordia Seminary awaiting their calls into the public ministry of the church. It was a moment of intense emotion when the dean read our names and our future fields of ministry. My call was to Southern California—to the church that turned out to be my first and last.

Long before this momentous event, I had been conditioned to accept God's call wherever it took me, and to give myself wholeheartedly to it. How this resolve came to me is, I think, an exciting human-interest story. That it would evolve as it did, was not even in my dreamiest imagination.

I was enrolled in a preministerial school in Oakland, Calif., when a good and faithful friend, Gustave A. Lau, staunch member of my father's church in Santa Rosa, Calif., gave me the opportunity to earn funds for my education. Those were the days when just about everyone welcomed opportunities to make good through a willingness to work. The odd thought of expecting security from others was not yet entertained to any appreciable degree.

In the community of Cotati, halfway between Santa Rosa and Petaluma, Mr. Lau had opened a general merchandise and feed store. This was the time when the famed chicken industry was developing in that area. The store supplied just about everything the ranchers needed. You could buy anything from canned peas to pitchforks. Even when some of the customers wanted gravel for the roads leading to their homes and barns, they were assured that their orders would be filled.

One day three carloads of gravel arrived and were placed on the rails alongside our warehouse. It was my job to empty these cars containing over 100 tons of gravel. This assignment offered me one of the most valuable lessons of my life. The shippers must have assumed that the gravel was to be used for the railroad bed, for they had put it into steel cars, called hoppers, with cantilever bottoms. Instead of being flat, the floor of each car was an up-and-down structure like a huge saw. This made shoveling distressingly difficult, since the worker never had a firm footing. The feet had to be planted on the downslope or the upslope, or both.

While thus engaged, with body askew, in the routine of lifting one heavy shovelful after the other over the 5-foot steel siding, I had time to do a lot of thinking. I kept thinking especially of my future life in the pastoral ministry. The prospect of mounting the pulpit and doing all the other work of the Christian ministry filled me with fear and trembling. These thoughts sent more beads of sweat to my forehead than did the work. A strong, new conviction was rising in my spirit. The Christian ministry must be something like shoveling that gravel, I thought: just a lot of hard work and a relentless struggle to get the job done. The words of Edison flashed into my mind: "Success is 99 percent perspiration and 1 percent inspiration." Though later experiences didn't always support this maxim when applied to the Christian ministry, I did learn a valuable lesson. The best way to get a job done is to do it. As the sweat dripped and the shoveling went on, I made up my mind in those gravel cars that I would make the sand fly in the same way for the Lord in whatever work He assigned. If I failed, it would not be due to a lack of willingness to work.

The Resolve Is Tested

It was in this mood and spirit that 6 years later I accepted my call into the Christian ministry in what was then known as the Manchester district of the rapidly growing city of Los Angeles. My vision of a paradise of palm trees, gardens, and flowers was rudely broken with the first glimpse of Manchester Avenue. The Red Car, running to the heart of the city from the Port of Wilmington, had just stopped in the community of Watts, destined in 1965 to gain national and worldwide attention through racial riots. I asked the man sitting next to me if he knew anything about the Manchester district. "Manchester Avenue will be our next stop," he answered. I tried to take in as much as possible of the area in which, as it turned out, I was to spend the next 44 years of my life. My heart sank at what I saw. An old truck had just pulled out of a brickyard near the station and was going down the unpaved avenue, leaving a huge cloud of dust around the ugly, dust-covered houses. To one who had just arrived from the verdant northern California countryside, especially the idyllic setting of Santa Rosa, this drab scene was a shock. I found later that things were not nearly as bad as the first impression indicated, for the center of my ministry was in a more attractive area some miles west of the section just described.

Now I would begin in earnest to put my gravel-car experience into practice. As there were no apartments available, and none of the handful of families that were to be my congregation had extra rooms, I took up residence at the Walther League hospice. Here I had good fortune to become acquainted with Mr. and Mrs. William G. Dettman, who managed the Lutheran hospice. I shall never forget the fun and fellowship in this home away from home. The sunshine of "Till" Dettman's personality, the fatherly interest of "Mr. D.," as we all addressed him, will always be remembered. Soon some of the young people living in the hospice were energetically involved in my work, serving as ushers and Bible school teachers. I truly enjoyed the year I spent with this fine group of Christian people.

Each day I spent the morning hours in the study room above the garage, a place prepared and equipped by my hospice friends. Every afternoon was given to visitations in the parish. Well do I recall the first of hundreds of such trips by streetcar. Eager to meet at least one person associated with the new group (soon to be known as Faith Lutheran Church of Los Angeles), I stopped at the one and only address I had, 8211½ Moneta Avenue, now called Broadway. Here I found a tiny one-room building of about

7 by 9 feet used as a real estate office by Mr. Alexius Colby (name has been altered), the secretary of the newly formed group I was to serve. His minutes deserve some kind of prize for their uniqueness. Here is a sample of one page in phonetic spelling to show how they were read: "De meedings fon Fate Ahwangehlikel Luddern Shurch vass held in de office of Alexius Colby, 8211½ Moneta Avenue, on Friday last month. It vass decide: 1. To do vhat Mr. Fredrickson said. 2. Not to do vhat Mr. Lebrecht said," and so on. Only the secretary's name and address came through loud and clear.

On that first visit I requested this gentleman to take me to the newspaper office to announce my first service as pastor. The service was to be conducted in an upstairs lodge hall of a ramshackle wooden structure known as Manchester Hall. Mr. Colby was ready to serve his new pastor, but for reasons of his own. He chose a circuitous route to show me various houses he was offering for sale. Brushing off every question relating to the church, he kept on extolling the merit of real estate deals he thought would be a good investment. I laughed to myself, as my earthly resources could hardly have been more than $20.

At the newspaper office I met the editor of the *South-west Topics,* a gracious and generous person who throughout the years gave our cause invaluable publicity. The following Thursday I was the editor's guest at a meeting of the Optimists, a service club of the area. Near the place where the Optimists met I saw the little theater where the first public worship service in the Manchester district had recently been conducted after the canvassing of the area by members of the local pastoral conference. Rev. August Hansen had come all the way from Pasadena for that Sunday afternoon service. When only one person showed up, he decided, after inner debate, to assert an action of faith rather than doubt by going on with the service. He noticed that his lone auditor did not show any interest in the service and did not appear to be listening to the sermon. If ever a man's faith received a blow it came when the pastor discovered that his audience of one was almost stone deaf! Nevertheless, that stoic audience of one person was the mustard seed destined to grow into a full-flowering congregation.

Rebukes Jar the Resolve

In the months that followed I kept faith with the "gravel-car resolve" by giving myself unsparingly to the work of the Lord. Most of the work was done by streetcar and on foot, for few of our people owned an automobile. One who did was Mr. Robert Fredrickson. He and his wife are valued friends and faithful working Christians to this day. Every Thursday I was a dinner guest in the modest home of Robert and Helen. After dinner the three of us would get into Bob's pickup truck to call on church prospects. Fortunately all of us had a good sense of humor; otherwise many of our experiences with people on whom we pressed the claims of the Lord would have brought only discouragement.

There was one man, whose intelligence threads were loosely held together, who demanded at least once a month that we explain to him why Martin Luther wrote the Catechism instead of using only the Bible. And there was the usher who chewed gum violently and winked at people while taking up the offering.

Sometimes we conducted our Sunday service amid the clattering of dishes being washed in the adjacent kitchen after a Saturday night dinner and dance. We had rented an upstairs hall from the Masons, who were in all other respects flawlessly cooperative. When one of their members who didn't like our line of work caused disturbance in the Sunday school, the Masons rebuked the offender and, after a second disturbance, cast him out of their ranks.

The Seed Grows

In the tiny seed placed in the ground, then quietly breaking forth into strong growth, Jesus saw an illustration of a Kingdom mystery. A routine experience sometimes shows this mystery at work today. In this case it was an ordinary ring of the telephone that started a process in which the Lord clearly had His hand.

I had just returned to the hospice on a Saturday noon after teaching a class of children in preparation for their confirmation. As the day was hot, I got myself into light clothes for an afternoon with friends at the ball game. A ring of the telephone abruptly changed my plans. I heard the weak voice of Catherine Miller, who was ill and wanted to see a pastor. Her own pastor had declined to visit her because of distance and the press of other duties. With a letdown feeling, I got back into more formal clothes and

into the streetcar for a hot 5-mile trip. In a meager room above a grocery store near Broadway and Slauson Avenues I met a middle-aged maiden lady who appeared extremely ill. I ministered to her spiritually and then inquired about her care. She had no one to care for her and had been too ill to prepare food for herself. Wanting to do for her what I would want her to do for me in like circumstances, I went downstairs, bought several cans of chicken soup, heated one of them, and spoon-fed the patient, who was too weak to feed herself. On the following Monday I found the patient much improved. I felt this would be about the last time I would ever see her, for she had her own church and pastor. I was quite wrong in this assumption, as it was this same Catherine Miller *who gave us a gift deed to a parcel of ground which became the site of our future church.* And it all began with an ordinary telephone ring on an ordinary day. Two cans of chicken soup plus a little love turned into a pretty fair investment.

As our worship meetings in Manchester Hall were being attended by growing numbers of people, it was apparent to all that we needed more room. In the kind of faith which was to characterize the group throughout the years, the decision was reached to build a church. On Aug. 7, 1927, the congregation had the high-peak experience of dedicating a beautiful church and parish hall. Going from rickety Manchester Hall to our new sanctuary was like moving from a hut to a castle. Though there were many other thrills to come, none ever matched this one. From now on our church was to grow in numbers and to widen its sphere of activity and influence.

Early Wanderings in "Gimmick" Land

We now had a beautiful church, a growing congregation, but also a church debt of $18,000. All of us were poor. Only one member had a new car. This member and his wife were old-time church people. Their weekly contribution of 50 cents was conspicuously the largest. Mr. and Mrs. William Joannes (name has been altered) were faithful in their attendance and undoubtedly sincere in their faith, but their thoughts about money were thoroughly secular. "God is interested only in saving our souls; He has nothing to do with our money," were the exact words of this well-meaning and lovable old gentleman. Yet this very person had more to do than he ever realized with the development of the pure and authentic stewardship principle which this book is all about.

I recall clearly how it happened. One evening this honored gentleman, whose estate was later bequeathed to the church, stood before the voters' assembly to suggest a method of gaining support for the Lord's work which, he said, had worked out well in his former congregation in the Midwest. He proposed that our congregation adopt the system which "worked like a charm back home." His home congregation annually published the names of members and the amount of money given by each during the year.

I squirmed uncomfortably at the suggestion, for only recently I had met a young man who was "offended out of his church" and was full of bitterness against it precisely because it published the names and contributions of its members. He told me that his widowed mother was a faithful contributor in this congregation, but the amount she was able to give made her look bad compared with amounts of wealthier members. "This thing is dishonest not in what it says but in what it doesn't say," he explained. "Giving out of her need, my mother's gift may have been a hundred times greater in God's eyes than the gifts of some, though the figures didn't show this." I had a feeling of sympathy for this young man. After hearing him out, I found myself attracted to his position rather than the one that was being proposed for our congregation.

My head was reeling with resentment against this plan and the sudden realization that its approval by our group was now a possibility. It was quite clear that Mr. Joannes' dignity and sincerity were effective in influencing opinion for his plan. Then something happened which to me was divine intervention. When a vote was asked for, the chairman of the meeting and president of the church, Mr. Leon W. Edson (whose faith and long years of service remain stamped upon the personality and spirit of the congregation), made a quick-witted suggestion, "It seems to me," he said, "that we ought to ask our pastor what he thinks of this plan." I knew then that Mr. Edson had spotted my uneasiness. Though I was thankful for a delay of the vote, and though I wanted to speak, I have to admit that a shudder of fright seized me. I didn't want to lose the affection of those who favored the plan, and I didn't want a plan that could offend people so much that they might leave the church.

If ever I had an experience of the truth of the Savior's promise that He will, through His Spirit, tell His children what to say when they get into difficult straits, it was that evening. *What I said must have come from God, for I had never engaged in such a line of reasoning before.* After my talk, all seemed to be on my side. The proposal was voted down. I felt that even the dignified Mr. Joannes voted against himself, though I am not sure. What I am sure of is that I was led by the Holy Spirit to say what I did. It went something like this: "It may be a good plan to publish the amounts people give to the Lord if this is done with complete honesty and fairness. Such honesty would direct us to publish the assets and liabilities of each member. A plan obviously intended to place a person's giving under the judgment of others must provide a true basis for such judgment lest it lead to untrue and uncharitable conclusions."

My little talk took hold. All seemed to consider it sincere and honest. One eager beaver was so impressed that he eagerly went beyond the scope of the original motion by adding the amendment "that we permanently decline to reconsider the plan."

A hurdle was overcome, but there were others. One of these was my own unsound, inadequate understanding of stewardship. I doubt that I had ever heard of the word, and I certainly did not know what it meant. There was no instruction on it in the seminary. The closest thing to it came as an informal remark by Dr. Francis Pieper in his final words to the class of 1925. In his quaint, humorous, yet profoundly sincere manner Dr. Pieper said, "Once the people in your congregation become sure that you are sincerely trying to prepare them for heaven, sausages will rain down upon you." Spoken in German the imagery has a tinge of humor which is missed in translation.

It has always been a mystery to me how a church could be so attentive to Christian doctrine and at the same time so remiss in its teaching of Christian stewardship. The prominence of this concept in the Scriptures is not matched by its prominence in the church, and for that failure the church is the poorer.

When the positives of Christian instruction are wanting, the negatives take over and have a field day. My trouble at this time was that I had no hold on the stewardship magnitudes of God's Word, nor did the other local pastors of my denomination. Nothing we heard, saw, or read opened our vision to the glory of the stewardship life. We had become so accustomed to financial deficits that we took them for granted. There was no radical, constructive plan to overcome them. So we plodded along, each trying in his own way to keep things going. Often the methods employed to accomplish this were thoroughly human and therefore consistently ineffective. Sometimes the methods were downright vicious.

Barbed-Wire Tactics

I remember the visit of one pastor who was widely

known for his skill in raising money. His tactics were cruelly clever. He employed the device of pitting one person against another, playing upon the human weakness to lust after status. The name and size of the gift pledged by the largest donor was placed at the top of a list of names displayed in the church narthex. This was obtained by psychological trickery. The potentially largest donor was driven to his decision by the suggestion that he set the pace. "When the first name and amount is on the list, it's in the bag," the pastor boasted. "Others will follow like sheep. Their miserliness is overcome by their desire to look good."

For the first time in my life I felt the anger that must have impelled Jesus to drive the money dealers out of the temple. This pastor quite forgot that God's work must be done in God's way. He was stacking the deck to win the game for the Lord, serving God by disservice, honoring God by dishonor. The words of Paul flashed into my mind: "An athlete is not crowned unless he competes according to the rules." (2 Tim. 2:5)

No person actually wins a race by cheating. *If it is God we are serving, we should let Him say how He wants to be served.* This understanding blazed its way into my spirit. As an insight it was neither exceptional nor profound, but it was the beginning of something better to come.

Tradition Dies Hard

Though there were some rays of light, we were still walking in the shadows. We were not yet ready to give up games and gimmicks to gain support for God's work. We knew that our Christian work program was right, and we made the error of thinking that nearly any method of gaining support for it would be right. We continued to do ridiculous things to raise funds for the greatest cause on earth.

A classic example came when one woman appeared before the ladies' aid with a plan to raise needed funds.

Lena Hunter (name has been altered), conspicuously the thinnest member of the group, took her position before the ladies with an enthusiasm that she hoped would be contagious. "Ladies," she said, "I have found a plan to help us raise money for the Lord's work." In order to catch the irony of this amusing incident, it should be said that the dimensions of most women present required large-size dresses. One member was lovingly dubbed "Mrs. Five by Five." Another weighed nearly 300 pounds. The group also included the sister of "Mr. Big," the 500-pound side-show attraction of the Ringling Brothers circus. His sister gave ample proof of her kinship. Reaching into her handbag, Lena extracted what appeared to be a long belt of heavy brown paper. "Ladies, I have here a money belt," she said, pointing to the belt that contained one slit per inch. "Now this is the way the plan works," she explained. "You take the belt home, insert a dime in every slit, and bring it back to the next meeting." Then came the payoff pitch. "Now you may wonder, ladies, how the length of the belt is to be determined for each of you. Well, that's the beauty of my scheme. You measure your girth (and no cheating, ladies), and then you put a dime into every pocket of as much of the belt as it takes to go around your waist."

I looked at Lena's waist, just a few degrees larger than a banana. Then I looked at the others, who would be required to pay much more than the one who made the proposal. I went into such a spasm of laughter that I had to stuff a handkerchief into my mouth and leave the room. The incident was hilarious, but the sting of its tragic principle remained long after the humor had worn away.

Under a gentle chuckle there remains a twinge of regret, even guilt, when I think of some of the meals served "to raise money for the church." One kitchen crew, eager to make a good profit, concocted a new recipe for meatballs with so much rice and so little meat that we all had a heaviness in the midriff that lasted long after the meal had been eaten. In addition, almost always there was an argument about the price of food tickets for children and adults. "Children eat as much as adults," lamented those who had no children, or only a few. They demanded a cost increase for parents with many children. But these parents felt they couldn't afford to attend at a cost they considered beyond their means, and naturally plugged for lower children's rates.

One witty chap in another church, resenting the lopsided ratio of bread over chicken in the chicken loaf, brought down the house and hurt some feelings when he put a barb into his speech. "The women of this church really know how to work miracles. Jesus could take a few fish and loaves of bread to feed 5,000 people, but these women too can do pretty well themselves. They can take 10 loaves of stale bread, throw in a few half-starved stewing hens, and feed 500."

Experiences like this raised nagging questions about the wisdom and the ethics of some practices going on in the church. Is it good to gain support for the church through all these devices? Couldn't the time and energy consumed by moneymaking ventures be better employed in projects and programs nearer the heart of the church's mission? Could it not be true that the women of the church who sweat out endless hours of hard work in putting on dinners, bazaars, and bake sales to realize a few dollars for the good cause would be far happier in ministries of Christian service that are more vitally linked with Christ's program of love? With profits so small and irritations so large, does it make good sense to continue these fund-raising pursuits?

Ecclesiastical Merchandising

Merchandising in the house of God is big business in America. Churches are exploited by commercial interests to provide a sales force to sell candy, fruitcake, plates, dishcloths, brooms, cosmetics, extracts, soaps, stationery, date books, and a lot of other things. *Is it morally right for the church, a tax-free institution, to compete with local taxpaying merchants?* These cross-country peddlers of merchandise want to do business in the community without paying local taxes as the businessmen do.

If the church is in deep financial troubles, a few bazaars or peanut sales will not save the Kingdom. The contention that the Lord gets a good deal out of these transactions crumbles under the question, "Does the Lord want such a deal?" It certainly is not what He has recommended. Buying and selling in the church displaces and defeats the kind of stewardship He has taught. That lesson we, in our young and financially troubled congregation, were about to learn.

Little Seeds of Stewardship

It was at this time that God was stirring awakenings in the soul of a man who was to lead us to a new understanding of Christian stewardship. To us, Kirk L. Page was the right man in the right place at the right time. Two graces qualified him for his task. He had the gift of a profound faith in the trustworthiness of God's Word. His faith was both childlike and mature. It was too sincere and honest to admit the possibility that God may not have said what He meant or meant what He said. And this man had the gift of a university-trained mind capable of cutting a path through an underbrush of fallacies.

One day Mr. Page came to my office to unburden himself of concerns that were heavy on his soul. "There must be a better way to gain support for God's work than the one we have been following," he said. "This poor, ineffective, beggarly way of serving the Lord of the whole world can't be right." He pointed out that our games and gimmicks, our constant appeals for funds were not successful but were, in fact, damaging. They were offending God and were depriving His children of the joys and blessings of serving Him on a higher plane.

I didn't need much convincing, as I had been doing some soul-searching myself. What I did need was the constructive proposal that together we research all the available sources and come up with some honest answers.

Our Quest Begins

First we would ask, "What is wrong with us? Where have we failed?" The Biblical story of the man who brought his epileptic son to Jesus prompted these questions. Jesus healed the boy after the disciples had failed. They asked, "Why couldn't we heal the boy?" They wanted to know where they went wrong. Ordinarily we are prone to ask, "What's wrong with others? What's wrong with the church?

What's wrong with the Synod? What's wrong with the church officials?" Usually we supply answers that put the blame on others, leaving us clean. We were not going to fall into that trap. *We were searching for truth to set us right and to set us free.*

Awareness of our failures grew intensely. We knew that we didn't have hold on the true and pure Biblical principle of stewardship, nor did it have hold on us. We were taking things into our own hands, out of God's hands. We were seeking His approval of our way, not our approval of His way. Only recently we had confronted our people with an appeal commonly used but ineffective and destructive. It went like this: "Upon analyzing the giving habits of our members, we find that a scant third are carrying the load while the others are getting by with giving little or nothing. The burden is falling on a few while the rest are going along for the ride." It didn't occur to us that we were implying and suggesting that giving to the Lord is after all a form of penalty. We ourselves, who were teaching others, were not yet sure that giving is a privilege. We wanted money more than the faith and love that yields it.

As we searched deeper, we found other flaws in the appeals employed to gain support for Kingdom causes. Sometimes these flaws were more than mere indiscretions; they were flagrant fallacies. There were appeals to pride, to shame, to good sportsmanship, to duty. There were some appeals to love and gratitude, but even these were sometimes used to incite shame. We were beginning to feel guilty and penitent for our many failures, and very sad because in this we had a lot of company. Reputable denominational leaders were as guilty as we.

Perhaps the most widely followed appeal, sound in appearance yet unsound in fact, is the common practice of challenging people to give to a budget. The budget, undoubtedly for good and worthy causes, is presented as a goal to be achieved. All who love God and His work are asked to assume their fair share toward attaining the budget. Thus a stewardship principle is invoked which is foreign to the one laid down by God. People are led to abandon the Biblical principle of giving in proportion to God's gifts. Instead, they are challenged to give in proportion to the budget. The high incentives are gone; the power has fled. Thus, without being aware of it, the church tears down what it wants to build up. Such contradictions are bound to lead to impotent stewardship ideas and practices.

Pure Stewardship Has Power

Though ways devised by men, however sincere, are found wanting, God's ways will never be found wanting. We were confirmed in that conviction. But we were not yet

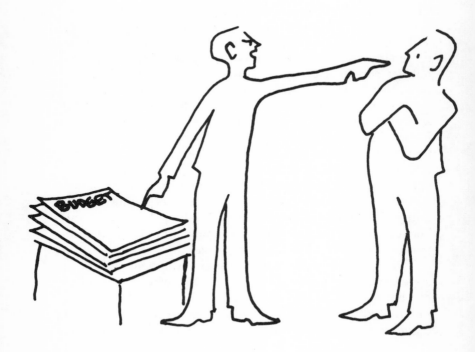

sure that we knew God's way. We were confident that God would never propose an unworkable plan for the promotion of His work. The plan He did propose, to be powerful and effective, must be kept as pure as He gave it. There should be no foolish attempt by men to improve on God's perfection.

An illustration of this truth was seen in the practice of the U. S. government as it held every incoming vessel at anchor for compulsory health inspection. Before these impatient ships are allowed to complete the last long mile to their piers, they must satisfy the vigilant authorities that they are not carrying contagious diseases to our shores. Health authorities know that a single virulent germ can devastate a city and bring on an epidemic.

This same kind of precaution is exercised by conscientious doctors as they prepare for an operation. Every doctor knows the danger to which the human body is exposed when an infectious agent enters it. We appreciate the wisdom of such precautions. They involve our individual welfare and that of our communities.

Shall we not have the same fear of becoming infected by impure ideas as by bad germs? Sound, pure, clean ideas and convictions are like good blood, the secret and source of health and vitality. Similarly, God's pure stewardship principles, without alteration or admixture with man's ideas, possess a vitality that proves their worth. *Positive, vital, inspiring stewardship truth always has power to set the spirit ablaze!* It will win friends and influence people, cutting its own channel into their hearts.

This was our experience when we started to put our convictions into practice. God's Word, whether on the subject of stewardship or any other subject, has power to make its way into human hearts. When God goes to work on a problem, it is on the way to being solved. As sunlight sends vermin scampering when rocks are overturned, so God's light drives away darkness. People were emerging from the shadows and coming into the light of a new understanding of the Christian life as a stewardship. Everywhere there was evidence of a new zeal for the work of the Lord. Manifestly, the Lord of the work was Himself directing it. As we ourselves had experienced the miracle of abundance through the stewardship life, so others were beginning to have the same experience. The constant prodding and pleading for funds and for workers was replaced by constant encouragement and appeal to claim the privilege and invite the blessing of living in stewardship faithfulness.

The miracle of stewardship is there for all to find and claim, but it will not come by doing nothing. The heart must do the hunting in faith and faithfulness. It is the seekers who will find, the askers who will receive, the knockers-at-the-door who will gain entrance into the house of promise and prosperity.

Each of the following chapters proposes to present an analysis of the larger aspects of the stewardship life. Problems are brought out into the open and their solution is, we hope, offered in a way that will lead to the blest quest for the miracle of the abundant life of Christian stewardship.

2

Stewardship — What Is It?

A Good Word Gone Bad

Stewardship is a beautiful word with a bad reputation. It has become a catchall for a lot of rubbish. Used for every imaginable type of money-raising scheme, it is a tired, tarnished word that has lost its luster.

Some have thought of giving up on the word altogether, fearing that the recovery of its early meaning is impossible. Terms to replace it, like Christian Estate Management, or Firstfruits Fellowship, or Firstfruits Withholding, are suggested. One thing is certain, this withered and infected yet noble plant named "stewardship" needs to be repotted, stripped of dead branches, fertilized, and exposed to the sun for new growth and flowering. If the paintings of the old masters merit careful restoration, there must be hope that "stewardship," a masterpiece of divine terminology, can be restored to worthy and honored acceptance.

If this is to be achieved, we shall have to get rid of the notion that stewardship is:

> A lever to pry money out of people,
> A seasonal spurt instead of a steady flow,
> An irksome duty rather than a privilege.

Only when pure and powerful stewardship positives take over will there be joy and hope in the society of the saints. The growth may be gradual, but it will be good. The word *stewardship* will again suggest springtime and flowers, seed and harvest, fertile fields and fruitful trees.

What, Then, Is a Steward?

We have often been told that a steward is a person who manages the estate of another. That answer is only partially right. In early Christian days the steward stood in close personal relationship with his master. Jesus speaks of a lord who told his stewards in effect: "Look, I am going on a journey. Now you take over in my place and do what you think I would want you to do." Given freedom to think for himself, the steward could act on his own initiative. He was trusted to run his lord's affairs with intelligence, judgment, honesty, aggressiveness. That gave honor and importance to the position.

We need to recover in our day these winsome and inviting shades of meaning. *We are free to choose how best to serve our Lord.* There is no compulsion other than a willing and loving loyalty to Christ and His cause. There is nothing legalistic about the arrangement between ourselves and our Lord. The Lord trusts us to do a good job, and we trust the Lord to show us His will and give us strength to do it.

This view is a million miles from the notion that stewardship means squeezing a few more pennies out of people. *Primarily stewardship is a very personal relationship between the steward and the Lord.* It is a matter of possessing, feeling, and expressing the loyalty of love that grows out of the joyful awareness of a partnership between ourselves and our Lord. This is implicit in the words of Jesus: "If a man love Me, he will keep My words; and My Father will love him, and We will come unto him and make our abode with him" (John 14:23). What an invitation to a precious partnership! Who can deny that this is an invitation rather than a browbeating attempt to impose behavior for the sake of "practical" results?

Children of a Sunday school were asked to explain stewardship in their own words. One child wrote: "Stewardship is the building of a service station on one's lot in life, wherever that lot may be." Another child said: "Stewardship means that life is like a great ship loaded with cargo to be delivered to many people in many places. God is the owner of the ship and its cargo, but He has made me the captain."

All that God has placed aboard the ship of life—time, talents, treasures, ability to think and to work—all is God's cargo to be delivered according to His will.

A Job for Angels?

The Lord Jesus Christ has made us His priests and stewards to deliver the salvation cargo to churches, schools, offices, homes, shops, factories, fields. Nearest His heart is the concern to bring people into His kingdom for life. This concern ought to be nearest our hearts, too. He has given us His Spirit and appointed us His partners in His mission of love. "As My Father hath sent Me, even so send I you" (John 20:21). The mere thought of the enormity of this assignment could trigger a shudder of fright. Why didn't He enlist a corps of angels for this work? He was certainly aware of the magnitude of the commission to cover the inhabited world with the news of salvation. He knew what vast resources of time, thought, energy, money, and skill the charge would demand. Yet He chose to assign this formidable mission to us. We who ourselves had received the salvation gift were to share it with all. Only those who had known the agony of sin's curse and the ecstasy of deliverance from this fiendish power could effectively tell others what they themselves had experienced. *Not even an angel could do that!*

Yet the Lord Christ did not ask us to venture for Him but with Him. He never expects His own to be completely on their own. His promise is to be with them until the end of time. In His work we are linked with Him in the closest bond of partnership. He has taken us into this most prized and costly corporation as junior partners. We are the ones who bring Him to men, but He is the One who brings men to Himself. We are merely tools in His hands, vessels meet for the Master's use. As His ambassadors our position is one of honor and trust, and we should regard it so. For this momentous task there is fresh courage in the knowledge that the Holy Spirit is speaking through us.

The voice is ours, but the message and the power are His. All we do is to administer the received gifts "as good stewards of the manifold grace of God" (1 Peter 4:10). We may always have some doubt as to our ability, but there should be no doubt about His ability. Whether we believe it or not, God has given us the gifts for His mission of love in the world. At one point He even said that we could do greater things than He did, but He never said that we could do them without Him.

Upon hearing an excellent speech or musical rendition or witnessing an athletic achievement by a person from whom we didn't expect it, we may say or think, "I never knew you had it in you." The talent and ability were there right along, but they had not been brought out. Similarly, there is in each of us a divinely given ability which God wants us to be aware of, to appreciate, and to use. It is nothing short of tragic that Christians are using only a small percentage of the gifts God has given them. *This means that fear is winning out over faith.* It must break the heart of Him who wants to use us for great purposes in His kingdom. We insist on doing the very opposite of what He is always asking of us, "Fear not; only believe."

Imitators of God

"We . . . reflect as in a mirror the splendour of the Lord . . . we are transfigured into His likeness . . . such is the influence of the Lord" (2 Cor. 3:18 NEB). Filled with God, we reflect Him. This is a helpful and important insight for a responsible person who wants to learn the full secret of the stewardship life. The God who indwells us is a loving and therefore a giving God. Everything in His world is always in a state of giving: the sun gives, the stars give, the fields give, the trees give, the flowers give, the oceans give, the lakes give, the rivers give. In his explanation of the First Article of the Apostles' Creed, Martin Luther sees God as the great Giver: "I believe that God has made me and all creatures; that He has given me my body and soul, eyes, ears, and all my members, my reason and all my senses, and still preserves them . . . that He richly and daily provides me with all that I need to support this body and life." David sang, "Blessed be the Lord, who daily loadeth us with benefits" (Ps. 68:19). Every loaf of bread and every piece of clothing is God's gift. We may pay for the process that brings these gifts to us, but the money we use to buy them is His gift.

Alongside earthly gifts there are the heavenly gifts. Here we think of the vast treasures of divine grace.

Physically and spiritually it is God who holds us in life. "In Him we live and move and have our being" (Acts 17:28). If God were to withdraw Himself from us for a moment, we would perish instantly. Once we understand our dependence upon God, we will grasp the wisdom of praying not for the gifts of God but for God Himself, the Source of every gift. *As there are no fruits apart from the tree that bears them, there are no gifts apart from the God who gives them.*

Belonging to a loving God who pours out His love to us and gives us all that He has to give, we are exhorted to be "imitators of God." As God gives and loves and serves, so should we. "Be ye therefore merciful, as your Father also is merciful" (Luke 6:36). It is precisely because giving makes us more godlike that "it is more blessed to give than to receive" (Acts 20:35). Giving is the language of love; it is godly language, for God is Love. Filled with the fullness of a giving God, we become givers ourselves. We give love, give thanks, give praise, give heed, give attention, give care, give time, give effort, give talents, give treasures, and even give forgiveness to others as He has given forgiveness to all. Thus we give proof that God has taken up His residence within us.

Good Trees Give Good Fruit

Jesus illuminated the stewardship secret when He said, "Every good tree bringeth forth good fruit; but a

corrupt tree bringeth forth evil fruit" (Matt. 7:17). A man, like a tree, can only be what he is, not what he is not. The adherents of non-Christian religions aspire to reach the goodness they desire; Christians aspire to express the goodness they have. Filled with the righteousness of the Kingdom and living under the reign of the King, they are like the "good man who out of the good treasure of his heart bringeth forth good things." (Matt. 12:35)

A good tree produces good fruit. It produces good fruit not because someone likes the fruit or because there is a demand for it but simply because it is a good tree. No amount of coaxing will cause the tree to produce better

ıre fruit. The successful fruit grower knows that
t and increased harvest depend on better trees.
ruth Jesus taught here is fundamental in steward-
ıows up the fallacy of thinking that all of a sudden,
aₜ ₋₋ ₂ck and call of the church, there will be a rich
harvest of fruit. Harvests never come that way. They come
in good time from good trees, in good soil, under good
nurture.

Nurture Is Necessary

Once in a dream, the story goes, a man encountered
an angel of the Lord. "I have run out of fruits of the Spirit,"
he said, "can you restock me?" Looking regretfully at him,
the angel replied, "I am sorry, we do not restock fruits,
only seeds." Life and harvest come out of the seed. The
mystery and miracle of growth in field and garden is in seed
and soil. The good seed in good ground under good growing
conditions promises a good harvest.

If we want to be good stewards, bringing forth good and
abundant fruit all our life, we will have to learn this deep
spiritual principle. "The seed is the Word," God says
(Luke 8:11). Christians are born into the new life out of the
seed of the Word. Through the Word the heavenly Gar-
dener cultivates and enriches the soil, nurtures the plant
in growth, stakes it against adverse winds, sprays it against
infestation, protects it from weeds, and brings it to flowering
and fruitage.

A Progressive Miracle

The good seed of the Word in the good soil of the believer's heart will produce a good harvest. This is a progressive process. This miracle goes on and on. The Chinese
have a saying, "You can count the number of seeds in an
apple but you cannot count the number of apples in a seed."
One apple containing ten seeds has the potential of pro-
ducing thousands of trees in a few years, and millions of

trees in a few decades. The believing steward understands the progressive miracle involved here.

Paul expressly applies the counterpart of this miracle of nature to the miracle of stewardship. "He who gives seed to the sower and turns that seed into bread to eat will give you the seed of generosity to sow and, for harvest, the satisfying bread of good deeds done. The more you are enriched by God, the more scope will there be for generous giving . . . resulting in an overflowing tide of thanksgiving to God" (2 Cor. 9:10-12 Phillips). *The miracle of stewardship, like the miracle of seed and harvest, is progressive.* The more one gives, the more one receives. He doesn't always receive in kind, but what he receives is more generous and precious than what he gives, for God's gifts are always better than ours. This doesn't make good sense in ordinary logic, but it is the kind of sense God has written into the stewardship mystery. Every faithful steward has experienced the truth of it, and many have publicly testified to its truthfulness.

Only God Can Work the Miracle

God is the secret and source of the stewardship miracle. All the gifts are from Him, the motivations to give are from Him, the cause to support is His, the promise to bless gifts and giver is His. Stewardship strength and success flow out of the union of God and the steward. Failure comes when God is edged out and the steward is left on his own. This is what frequently happens, and it explains the failure of many stewardship efforts. It simply isn't smart to tell God to get out and stay out of a process which depends on Him for success.

We don't like to admit this. We may not be aware of it at all. But this is exactly what is done in man-made stewardship appeals: If we want to get results, we will have to get them our way—and God better stay out of the way. He is too idealistic and His method is too unrealistic for this kind of job. This process touches the "business" of the church; it calls for approved business techniques and highly organized campaigns. When it comes to promotions and business, we'll get better advice from Madison Avenue advertising agencies than from God. The money promoters have become so efficient that they no longer need the help of the Holy Spirit; they can do it on their own. All God has to do is to approve what we are trying to do for Him, no matter how much this is in conflict with what He wants. We need Him for color, not for counsel; for decor, not for direction.

When it comes to business, even if it is His, we presume to know more than God does. So we get Him out of the way because He stands in our way. And what is *our* way? Our way is to insert a human element between God and the steward. We are certain that motivations for giving provided by us are better than those provided by God. We have little confidence in God's ability to motivate His children. We can do better.

And so we get to work with our ideas. We set goals, devise catchy motivations, organize high-power campaigns, bombard people with appeals, and get our show on the road. If God cares to, He can look in from the outside. Our main interest is in the *size* of the offering, not in its source. We want cash at any cost. We don't realize that the cost may be much greater than we can afford. We don't stop to think that our way may cause the permanent loss of the good will and good stewardship of sensitive and sincere Christian people. The "crisis" of today is the important issue—tomorrow can wait.

Such campaigns may gain temporary results in cash, but they lose more than they gain when they fail to strengthen the spiritual convictions that nurture the long-range stewardship life. In building up the superstructure we break down the foundation. Even from a utilitarian point of view the folly of tampering with the spiritual inner mechanism of a sensitive steward should be apparent. What sense is there in gaining $500 for the present and losing a potential $5,000 or even $50,000 in the future? It just doesn't make good sense. God knows it, but we don't seem to. God is always trying to teach us wisdom, but we want to be the teacher, not the pupil.

If the motivations for giving are not right, then the giving will not be right. This was in Paul's mind when he said that giving should not be "of necessity" or "grudgingly" but "cheerfully" (2 Cor. 9:7). A person should not be told to give a cent until he wants to, and that will be when the Holy Spirit tells him to.

God looks behind the gift to the motive. So should God's church. Instead of being happy with falsely motivated gifts, the church should insist that it desires no gift on the Lord's altar from an unwilling heart. Churches employing pressure techniques for funds are breaking down the true stewardship principle on which their success depends. Thus they are sawing off the limb that holds them up. They are blasting the foundation on which they stand.

We need again to see stewardship in its true beauty and nobility. *The idea that it is a device to get something out of people must be thoroughly rejected.* It is God's way of getting something into people, for their enrichment, something noble and beautiful and good and true and enduring. Through the stewardship life God is trying to make them:

> A channel of blessing to many,
> His partners in getting the Word to the world,
> Builders of an eternal kingdom,
> Investors in an eternal estate.

Persuasion from Within or Pressure from Without?

These choices come into play, and we must choose between them. Here we stand at the fork of the road. It must be one way or the other. We cannot successfully take two directions at the same time. When it comes to choosing a stewardship life for ourselves, we will have to decide whether the direction should be from the inside out or the outside in.

Christian theology has, of course, already given the answer. On our own, God expects nothing of us except failure. Jesus made that quite clear when He said, "Without Me ye can do nothing" (John 15:5). Every demand God makes upon us is a demand upon His grace within us. The Bible never departs from this fundamental position. We grow in holiness, not into holiness. It is not a case of working our way into God's grace, but of God's grace working its way in us and through us.

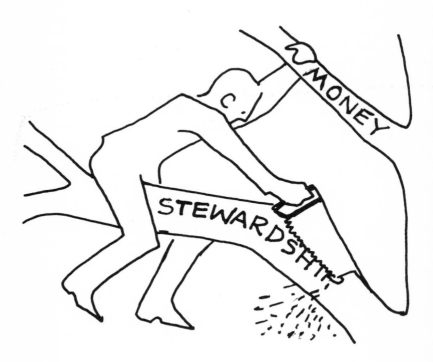

To be sure of our ground here we need to answer this critical and decisive question: "Which is the stronger force, the love of Christ and the power of the Holy Spirit urging us to use the grace we possess, or some kind of pressure from the outside?" One church member answered the question this way: "Since becoming a member of your church I have given more to the Lord in one year than I gave in any five years previously." He went on to explain: "Formerly I was put under so many pressures that I began to resist them. After coming into your church I felt free for the first time in my life to make my own decision, and for the first time I made a decision that really expressed my faith, my love, and my sincere and conscientious conviction."

The usual pressure devices are vulnerable. They succeed in gaining some money, but they also succeed in stopping a Christian from growing into stewardship maturity. As God's love is constant, not seasonal, so the mature steward, driven by that love, will be constant in his love and in his proof of that love. There is something fictitious about love that is turned off and on. The love the Holy Spirit nurtures is the love that is consistent with the day by day outpouring of God's love. Without this promise, the "Christian" life can, and does, become a drudgery, having only form and being void of joyful reality.

The Steward's Liberty and Responsibility

The word *responsibility* comes from the Latin *responsus,* meaning response. It stands for a man's response to some honor bestowed, some blessing received, some privilege given. A responsible steward is free to show appreciation of his privileges. The church may guide him, challenge him, teach him, encourage him to a decision in proportion to his blessings, but only he can make the decision which is right for him. It should be a decision out of his own faith and his own conscience. He must remain free to make it for himself under God. No one has the right to invade the private sanctuary of another's heart and mind. The decision should be one the steward can live with in good conscience, one he can practice in good faith, and one he can express in faithful love. *Under no circumstances should a person be driven to a decision which he is not willing or ready to make.* The person or church which tells another how much to give presumes to supplant another's faith, conscience, and liberty. This discourages a member from thinking things through for himself and seeking God's will as it applies to himself only. God alone can tell a steward how to administer His affairs. Any wedge driven between the steward who loves God and God who loves the steward is offensive to God and hurtful to the steward.

The faithful God and the faithful steward working together—that's the winning combination. No one can improve on that. If a man is as faithful in his stewardship as God is in His gifts and promises, failure is impossible, success inevitable.

3

Ingredients for Joyful Stewardship

Stewardship cannot exist in isolation. It is a reservoir fed by many streams, a cable of many strands, a diamond of many facets. Born out of the heart of God, energized by faith, sustained by hope, inspired by love, nurtured by the Spirit, this holy virtue weaves into the tapestry of time the record of a richly productive life.

The church is beginning to understand, though comprehension is often lamentably slow, that more attention needs to be given to the inner spiritual springs, the life in the Spirit, from which the streams of stewardship living and practice flow.

The Joy of Worship

To the question, "What is the chief end of man?" the Westminster Catechism has this renowned answer: "To glorify God and to enjoy Him forever." The worship of God is man's noblest work. Joyful in its very nature, worship should be regarded as our primary privilege. In contrast to other activities which become means to ends, worship is an end in itself, the beginning of something we shall be doing eternally. The word worship is a contraction of worth-ship. When we worship, we show God's

worth. *Our stewardship of life will be as high or as low as our appraisal of God's worth.*

Worship gives creative fulfillment to life. Without it a vacuum remains at the center. We have often heard but perhaps less often understood St. Augustine's profound words, "Thou, O Lord, hast made us for Thyself, and we shall not find rest until we find it in Thee."

As the therapy of work declines through more leisure, and the inspiration of worship recedes, man's struggle against boredom will increase. The experience of a sense of meaninglessness, emptiness, futility, and absence of direction on the part of millions of otherwise normal people is due to the loss of the divine presence. The further a man gets away from God, the further he gets away from himself and from his fellowmen. The loss of spirituality in a day of technology leaves only the deadly neutrality of boredom. This will continue until a person discovers that the supreme use of his time, talents, and wealth lies in the worship and service of God.

Except for worship, the angels in heaven would be afflicted with boredom. Life for us becomes lustrous with purpose and meaning when we claim our position as sons of God and take our place alongside the adoring angels who are always offering their jubilant doxologies to Him who is "worthy to receive glory and honor and power" (Rev. 4:11). Abandoning the service of God for the service of self, we soon become dissatisfied with ourselves, with others, and with life in general. In serving self we miss the service of God; and when God is missing, the essential meaning of life is missing. *Life without God is not life at all but mere existence.* The worship and service of God is life; the service of self is a slow process of death. It has few rewards, and none of them is lasting. On the other hand, a soul vibrating with the praise of God, thankful for the care of God, zealous for the honor of God is "a well of water springing up into everlasting life" (John 4:14). Joy comes to life when God instead of self is the object of love and worship. The orchestration in the natural world of sound, color, fragrance, growth, and beauty has its counterpart in the symphony of the spiritual world when the inner being of man bursts forth in the praise and glorification of God, finding high delight in God's world of grace and love and truth and peace and joy.

The person who has the worship of God in his heart will show it not only in words but also in the works of his hands and in the love errands of his feet. The offering we bring to God each Lord's day is an act of worship just like confessing the Creed, singing the hymns, hearing the sermon, and engaging in prayer. *The spirit of worship and the spirit of stewardship are cut of the same cloth,* and they have essentially the same purpose, to express the infinite magnitude of God's worth to us, to tell Him how great we think He really is. To avoid this worship of God, whether in word or deed, is to flirt with danger to the soul. It's like putting a frog into a tub and gradually adding hot water; without noticing it, the frog will eventually be cooked to death. A Christian who deserts worship is gradually but surely dying spiritually by inches without realizing that death is taking place.

The Joy of Living in Love

Dedication to a great cause makes a great life. The love of God, inspiring a burning zeal to share that love with a world that will die without it, gives the greatest motive for the adventure of Christian love. Paul sang, "Thanks be to God, who in Christ always leads us in triumph, and through us spreads the fragrance of the knowledge of Him everywhere." (2 Cor. 2:14 RSV)

As people on their way to "sharing the glory of God," the early believers walked the glory road of loving service to mankind. Their vigor, productiveness, and zeal grew out of their faith in the positive worth of their mission to transform the world through the love of God in Christ Jesus.

There was something contagious about the way they thought and acted. People saw a splendid new power at work in them, and they longed to understand it and experience it for themselves. It was their delightful enthusiasm that made them conspicuous and attractive.

The word enthusiasm, derived from two Greek words meaning "in God," may have been coined to describe this unique phenomenon. They were wildly excited about what they had found, an island of peace and love in the turbulence of their world. "By this shall all men recognize you as My disciples, that you love one another," their

Lord had said (John 13:35). And all who looked upon them were amazed to "see how they love one another." Caecilius wrote, "They know one another by secret marks and signs, and they love one another almost before they know one another."

The 20th-century Christian will recapture the early power and enthusiasm when he recovers the first-century love. This is not out of the question, for love is God's gift in our day as much as in that day. In contending for the preservation of the early Creed, Christians need to contend as faithfully for the preservation of the early love.

"Owe no man anything but to love one another," was Paul's radical and essential approach to every church problem (Rom. 13:8). *The conspicuous want in the modern church is the virtue of love.* "Our churches would be filled to the overflowing if people were sure that they would find love in them," was the considered assessment of Dwight L. Moody. The person who enters a Christian assembly with the resolve to express his debt of love to the God of love and to the people whom God loves will be a Kingdom-builder, never a Kingdom-breaker. The person who shows by his attitude, his words and actions, that he has no love for his fellowmen in his heart proves that he has no love in his heart for God. One such loveless individual can break up more churches, ruin more ministries, destroy more Christian projects and programs, hurt more feelings, than the worldling who never darkens the door of a church and has no power to darken its light. The worldling adds darkness to darkness, but the loveless "Christian" adds darkness to light.

Nothing will make the Christian cause so attractive as love in action. The living sermon of love is our most effective witness to the living Lord of love. Many people who give up on the church are not so much overcome by doubts about the teachings of the church as by lack of evidence that those within love one another, without which all dogma is nothing. St. Paul would tell us in our day, as he did in his, that without love all our stewardship activities are nothing, but then he would add that without stewardship our love is nothing more than myth and fiction.

The Joy of the Redemptive View of Life

To be himself, as a new creation of God, man must love. Love is the essential character of the new self. God has created, redeemed, and sanctified us for love. By sending His Son on a rescue mission for our redemption, God expressed His redemptive love for us. Under the power of redemptive love we belong to God and we belong also to the people whom God loves.

Now we as stewards are bearers of God's redemptive mission. Having been lifted to the high ground of peace with God, and having tasted freely of the waters of life, we cannot choose to dam up the river against those down below living in the desert of despair and unbelief.

Someone through the loving use of his time and talents brought us the good news about God paying our huge sin debt. It is now our turn to share the good news with others. Paul regarded himself a debtor to all. Our debt is threefold. We are indebted to God for paying off our debt; we are indebted to those who brought us the good news of the fully paid debt; we are indebted, as possessors of God's love, to share it with those who will die without it.

Christians resent the Marxist charge that religion is the opiate of the people, but they had better try to learn what opiate it is that deadens the Christian concern to release Christ's redemptive love in the world. Is the Christian church refusing to pay its debt to God, to its forebears, and to the world? God gave us the money, God gave us the ability, God gave us the time; but we have often failed to use, or have selfishly misused, His gifts. Every un-Christianized area in the world is a charge against us. So is every struggling mission field and undermanned institution. Money spent on extravagances and personal luxuries will rise against us in the day of judgment if given precedence over the withholding of God's share for His redemptive mission.

Self-Examination Recommended

What is the trouble? How can good people be so bad? How can sincere Christians have so little heart for what is nearest to the Lord's heart? There must be a reason. If we are looking for sincere and honest answers, we will soon find ourselves under self-judgment. If there is one area in which Christians had better judge themselves before they will be confronted with God's judgment, it is in their lack of zeal for their redemptive mission. Why is this? Is it true that the measure of interest we have in the salvation of others is precisely the measure of interest we have in our own salvation? We had better get honest-to-God and honest-to-self answers to this question: *"Why am I not more zealous and faithful as a steward in fulfilling my redemptive mission?"*

"Do I not have the joy of God's peace in my heart? Does it mean so little to me that Christ has given me peace of heart and peace of mind? Doesn't it thrill me that the evil foes lie at His feet—sin and its curse, death and its darkness, hell and its terrors? Does it mean so little to me that there is no further need in my life for fear, doubt, anxiety, despair? Can't I understand or don't I believe that for my sin there is forgiveness; for death, life; for hell, heaven; for despair, hope; for anxiety, faith?"

It was this sterling quality of peace that made the early Christians so zealous for their cause. Theirs was the serenity of a great peace coupled with the concern of a great love. It was this divine peace in the heart of Paul, in contrast to his previous anxieties, that wrought in him the compulsion for a demanding program of service to humanity. Shod with the Gospel of peace, his feet carried him across two continents to proclaim the Gospel of peace. This peace fascinated his mind, filled his spirit, fortified his heart. "We are handicapped on all sides," he wrote, "but we are never frustrated; we are puzzled, but never in despair. We are persecuted, but we never have to stand it alone; we may be knocked down, but we are never knocked out! . . . Always 'going through it,' yet never 'going under!' . . . We are penniless, and yet in reality we have everything worth having" (2 Cor. 4:8-9; 6:9-10 Phillips). The very peace that brought serene calm to his soul made him restive to share it with others. We can understand why without the peace of God people throw away their lives, but it is difficult to understand how a person who has the peace of God in his heart can refuse to give his life to God on the redemptive road.

Perhaps we have failed to understand the true character of the peace that God gives. It is not the peace of the contented cow but of the valiant warrior. It does not render us immune to the world's pain, but has precisely the opposite effect. If a man has love in his heart, if his scales can weigh the anguish of tears, he will be alive with concern to share his joy and his peace and his hope with those who are living under the tyranny of dreadful masters.

At peace with God and with himself, a man becomes a bearer of vast inner wealth, and he longs to share it. Liberated from fear, he is free to help dispel the fears of others. From now on he will not say, *"I have so little I cannot afford to give much,"* but *"I have so much I cannot afford to give little."*

The Joy of Worthwhile Achievements

Every Christian should try to be the person God intended him to be. "Ye are the salt of the earth" and "ye are the light of the world," Jesus said (Matt. 5:13-14). Salt and light penetrate. Salt drives out impurity, and light dispells darkness. If, however, salt loses its saltiness and light is covered up, both become useless.

When a redeemed man with all his potentials and almost limitless possibilities allows himself to degenerate into uselessness, he becomes savorless salt and a covered light. This is the tragedy of life in which self instead of God is the object of service and worship. When a person loses the grace which makes him a blessing to his fellowmen, he is good for nothing. It was Jesus Himself who led us to that kind of thinking. Savorless salt, He said, is "good for nothing." Fruitless vines will be cut off and cast into the fire. *The Lord Jesus could no more endure denatured personality than savorless salt or hidden light.*

Neither God nor we ourselves can long stand a life that has no worthy and meaningful spiritual achievements. No amount of service to self can permanently provide zest for living. Though a fat bank account and a variety of luxuries can bolster up the ego for a while, sooner or later the emptiness and bankruptcy of such a life is apparent. This happens every time a person discovers, as he will eventually, that there is immense futility and meaninglessness in a life that goes nowhere, helps no one, and achieves nothing worthwhile and enduring.

No person who is faithful to the Holy Spirit can regard himself as useless and valueless after he has seen how precious the redemption of the human soul from death to life really is. Not until we understand the tragedy of the eternal loss of the human personality will we cease putting a low value on self and trifling with life as a sacred trust.

Time, for What?

If life is a sacred trust, so is the time upon which life feeds. It is God's intention that His children weave into the fabric of time worthwhile activities in the service of God and mankind. God wants us to fill every new page of life with singing faith, joyful praise, radiant hope, loving service.

Boredom vanishes when earthly hours are filled with the music of life attuned to the ecstasies of eternity. In terms of everyday living this means that a Christian steward is never off duty. There is no time when he is excused from service to his Lord. This does not mean that we must always be on our knees repenting, praying, or reading the Bible. It means that, wherever we are or whatever we are doing, we belong to God and are in His service. It is this inner attitude of having a mind and a heart for God and His cause that goes with us like our shadow, whether it be to a ball game, an outing, a picnic, or a social gathering.

St. Paul reminded young Timothy that he was a soldier of Christ and that a good soldier never got himself "entangled in the affairs of this life, that he may please him who enrolled him as a soldier" (2 Tim. 2:4). Christ enrolls real soldiers, not tin soldiers, in His army. A genuine soldier will not lay down his arms in the midst of battle to chase butterflies.

As Christian stewards we may not choose to do with our time what we wish. Time, like money, is precious, but unlike money we cannot store it up. We can use it only when it is there. Time is like a flowing river; one can never step into the same water again.

One of the immense tragedies of our day lies in the loss of the vast resources of time available to Christian men and women which is not being administered for Christ and Christian service. Arthur Brisbane, whose syndicated column appeared in hundreds of daily newspapers, had this sharp observation: "The greatest loss to the human race has not been caused by floods or by fire, nor by epidemics which have spread diseases over vast areas and with the sickle of death mowed down millions, nor by earthquakes and tropical storms, nor by record-breaking crashes on Wall Street . . . *the greatest loss has been in the buried talents of God's people.*"

Intelligent and alert stewards who view the present in terms of eternity will wisely provide safeguards against all wanton waste of time. When Christians shrug off Christian work on the "I have no time" pretext, they perhaps would be stating the case more honestly by saying, "I am not willing to set aside any time for God." The work we refuse to do, though God has given time and talent for it, cannot be done by anyone else in exactly the same manner in which our own God-given talents lead us to do the work. No two people have talents exactly alike. "If two of us were exactly alike," a humorist remarked, "one of us would be superfluous." Moreover, if another person is required to do our work for us because we refused to do it, that person is unable to do the work which God has cut out for him and his talents. God has distributed time and talents for the common enrichment of the Christian community. *The congregation will be poorer for every given talent withheld.*

Christians should be as much concerned about the proportionate giving of time as of treasures. Only strict and heroic discipline can preserve us from the TV hypnosis which spellbinds Americans for an average of 35 hours a week. Perhaps many of these would invoke the "I have no time" plea if asked to give the Lord an honorable share of their time.

No church should operate with a goal lower than having every redeemed man and woman and child in the Kingdom enlisted in some form of Kingdom work. All powers of our personality have been redeemed by a divine Savior, and they belong to Him, to be used according to His will and to His glory. When a man believes that, and tries to act upon it, he becomes radiant with power and aflame with a desire to share in the reclaiming of mankind through the message of redemption and a life filled with service to God and man.

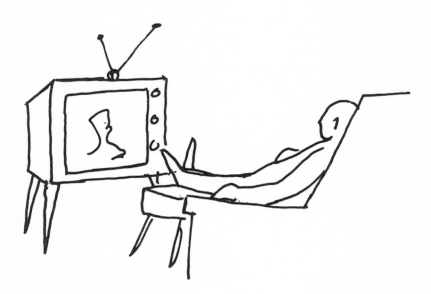

4

Why People Give and
Why They Do Not

The good stewards one meets shy away from efforts to psychoanalyze their reasons for following the stewardship way. There was no single factor, they say, that led them to the stewardship decision. It was rather a combination of light beams that one day focused on the inner response mechanism, tripping the switch from "off" to "on." About 50 such people checked a questionnaire in this order:

I decided to be a good steward because:
1. I want to show my gratitude for all God has done for me.
2. I want to be faithful in my stewardship.
3. I want to live within God's will.
4. I want my life to count for God.
5. I want to be true to God's principle to give as He prospers.
6. I want to lay up treasures in heaven.

These same people, reflecting their own struggle before achieving a breakthrough to the stewardship way, checked some hurdles which had to be overcome:

1. I can't afford to be a good steward.
2. I have to take care of myself first.

3. I intend to give when my ship comes in.
4. I was not taught as a youth to give percentage-wise.
5. Constant appeals for money led me to hold back in expectation of the next appeal.

Some of these good stewards accepted our invitation to show how they came over to the stewardship way:

"In the early years of our marriage we were afraid to give much to the Lord, as we were barely able to make ends meet between paydays. Our new life in stewardship began under the inspiration of a sermon by Dr. Erwin L. Kurth, who helped us muster up enough nerve to begin taking ten percent off the top of our modest stack of greenbacks. To our amazement we had money left over when the next payday rolled around. It has been that way ever since. . . . Sometimes when we get an extra-large paycheck we are happy that God's share is now larger than our entire monthly income was before. The secret is to take God's share off the top. This is the only way we know that keeps the love of the almighty dollar under control. We now find that however we invest our dollars which are left over and above the tithe, something good always follows, and we are sure that the Lord plans it that way."

MR. AND MRS. FRED DIETRICH

"Having grown up under the influence of parents who believed that the least possible gift of love and gratitude to God was the tithe, given not under duress but with the joy of returning the firstfruits to the Giver of all good gifts, I have had ample proof over and over again that never does the Father forsake one who complies with this principle of stewardship. He does open the windows of heaven to pour out immeasurable blessings which can come to the heart in realizing the importance of seeking first the kingdom of God and His righteousness.

EVANGELINE ELLINGSON

"My development in stewardship was a sort of three-pronged affair. First, there was the spirit and practice of my mother, a true Hannah in Israel. Although we were a poor family, Mother saw to it that as soon as we children started to earn money, a respectable amount was set aside for the Lord. My second step came when a very dear friend of mine, a person with whom I attended school, opened my eyes to the glory and meaning of proportionate giving. My third step came through the example and gentle instruction of my good friend W. C. Dickmeyer, who has been a tither most of his life and in late years went far beyond the tithe. . . . From personal experience I found that you cannot outgive God. . . . Regardless of what my contributions were, they were returned to me even before I had a chance to pay off my commitments."

ERNEST J. GALLMEYER

"Faith Church helped us to discover the mighty miracle of stewardship. In former years we thought ourselves poorer for giving to the Lord, but now we know that we are richer for doing so. We have found that the more we give to the Lord, the more He gives to us. We cannot explain how this can be true, but it is true. As far as we are concerned, it is just a plain miracle, but we have experienced it constantly since becoming stewards. This is not our motive for being good stewards, but we definitely know that this is a result of being so."

MR. AND MRS. RICHARD WENDT

"To us the stewardship way of life is the only way that is right. Jesus said, 'Every branch in Me bringeth forth fruit.' We are convinced that every person who is in union

with Christ, the living Vine, will be a fruit-bearing Christian. To us it is wonderful to think of ourselves as channels for Christ, with a heart, a mind, a will which does not choose to block Christ out in unbelief but is open and yielded to Him in seeking and doing His will. We are thankful beyond words in the knowledge that Christ is using us for great and true purposes in His cause."

MR. AND MRS. WALTER KRAUSE

"Until I was almost 30, I gave little thought to joining the church. My thinking, and that of many of my friends, was—if the church has so much to offer, why must it so constantly beg or put the pressure on its members for money to support it? Why don't the members support it voluntarily and joyfully because they love it and believe in it? Then I married a wonderful Lutheran girl and joined her church. I soon learned that the church did have so much to offer, that my deep-seated objections to the constant emphasis on money-raising by poorly motivated methods should never cause me to forfeit the true riches offered by our generous and loving Lord. My latent desire to find a better way was born but lay dormant until we became members of the author's church and, as he recounts in his book, began to put our faith in the stewardship mystery. After 40 years I can truthfully say that one of the greatest joys of my life has been the privilege of working with him intermittently through the years on stewardship ventures.

"His book offers the long-evaded answers to this problem of sustaining and promoting the work of the Kingdom. He advocates, and I strongly agree, the continuous teaching of God's stewardship instructions and faith in His promises. He rejects the reliance on appeals to pride, shame, duty, or organized solicitation of gifts and confrontation of members instead of enlightened free choice to give 'as a man purposeth in his heart.' My wife and I gladly testify that our Lord has never broken a promise to us and that the rewards of our stewardship living have been truly satisfying."

MR. AND MRS. KIRK L. PAGE

"It is my conviction that the Sealed Pledge, coupled with constant instruction in the stewardship way of life, is the best way to win friends and influence people for Christian fruit-bearing. Few things will offer so much inspiration to a person's spirit as to know that through his stewardship he is sharing the love of Christ with others."

ALFRED G. ZEISLER

"I praise my God and Lord that He has honored me to be His very own. In a very special way I thank Him for my parents and their example of Christian living. With them God was first, and their stewardship faithfulness has been a light for their children. I try to be a faithful steward to show my gratitude to God for sending His Son to die for my sins and the sins of the world.

WALTER BUEHLER

"I am thankful that the Lord led me into stewardship early in life by the example of a Christian mother who taught me to tithe my income from the very beginning. My stewardship life was strengthened in Faith Church through the use of the sealed pledge and the practice of percentage giving. In this I have found joy and freedom. A person need never be afraid to give generously. As salvation makes us free in the grace of God, even so faithfulness in steward-ship gives us a feeling of joyful freedom in showing love to God."

DR. T. S. HARRIS

"My spirit is filled with praise to God for the boundless blessing of being a child of God by the Holy Spirit, who wrought faith in my heart. The confidence that I am on the way to eternal glory gives me unspeakable joy and peace. I know that whatever talents and material blessings I have flow from His loving-kindness. That I am now His steward, that I find it a joyful privilege to use my life and all I have as a ministry to my fellowmen and to the glory of Christ — all this I regard as His very special grace. Praise be to His holy name!"

CLARENCE AMLING

"To be chosen by God in His marvelous grace and to be honored to become a partner with Him in faithful stewardship living fills my heart with love and gratitude toward Him. In worship, praise, and thanksgiving I place the fruits of the labors of my hands on His altar that His

Word may be sent where my feet cannot go, where my voice cannot be heard, where my hands cannot serve."

MRS. JOHN HARTMAN

"I say this humbly but truthfully and with deep gratitude to God. Some years ago I gave God only a dollar or two a month; now I try to give Him at least $100 out of a salary of $800. This has given me more joy in my faith than I ever had before. I am convinced that faith honors God and God in turn honors faith. In His ministry on earth Jesus honored faith wherever He found it. He was always able and willing to help people who put their faith in His promises. It is my hope and purpose, if God continues to bless me in the future as He has in the past, to return to him $200 or more a month for the cause nearest my heart and nearest His heart too."

ANONYMOUS

Every convinced and working steward is anxious to assist his fellow Christians to the experience of the stewardship power. What amazes, and often discourages, him is that others seem so reluctant to buy the product that he is sold on. He has discovered what he regards as a key to abundance, and his friends will not even try it out to see if it will unlock treasure secrets for them. He would not give it up for anything, while they would not give anything to try it out. Why is it that some are so set on stewardship while others seem so set against it?

As there are ingredients that lead to joyful stewardship, so there are roadblocks that prevent it. Understanding what these roadblocks are, we shall be better equipped to avoid them ourselves and help others overcome them.

A False View of Security

The desire for financial security often stands in the way of wholehearted commitment to the stewardship life.

By giving what they consider too much to the Lord, people fear that they will have what they consider too little left for themselves. Every Christian should come to a realistic and God-pleasing philosophy on the security issue. There is undeniably a legitimate striving for personal security. This is as natural as the instinct for self-preservation. Man's concern to make himself secure against the demands and trials of life is not wrong in itself. There is, however, a striving for security which is itself a sign of, as well as a sure way to, insecurity. Under the guidance of the Holy Spirit, the Truth-teller, we should learn the difference between the true way and the false way to security. The true way is that we acknowledge our dependence upon God for the kind of security that really makes us secure. The real security stands firm and remains constant when every other kind fails. Only God gives that kind of security, for

only He can keep us from falling and failing. *Without God no man can be secure, though he may possess millions.* Only on the ground of faith in His promise that He will deal with His beloved and believing children according to His wisdom and love can a man say with perfect confidence: "In spite of the hazards and uncertainties of life which I face every day, I am confident that nothing can reach me unless it first passes Him whom I know and trust as my Father and Friend."

Real and Unreal Values

In the materialistic view the real values are those which are seen. It is to describe those values that man has invented the term real estate. God, however, never uses that term in the sense we do. From God's point of view the term is false and misleading. In the world of secular economics the earth to which a man holds title is a solid basis for credit and for sound economic collateral. Insofar as their life touches the world of everyday business, Christians too operate with that principle. We must be careful, however, that our thinking is not so grossly adjusted to earthly economics that we render ourselves incapable of accepting God's way of security. Living in the climate of materialism, we may find it difficult to give unqualified endorsement to God's clearly stated truth that the unseen values are real whereas those that are seen are often not real, being as temporary as the grass of the field.

God says that we cannot find life in earthly possessions. Why not? Because for life we need God—His grace, His love, His forgiveness, His care. These values offer the foundation for true security. *Not the fragile arms of economic support but the everlasting arms of God are strong enough to sustain us.* This is the truth that sets a person free from the tortures of doubt, the fear of the loss of security, the delusion of trust in earthly riches.

God is trying to lead us to the wisdom of putting our confidence in values that will never give way. This is what Paul had in mind when he said: "Our eyes are fixed, not on the things that are seen, but on the things that are unseen: for what is seen passes away; what is unseen is eternal" (2 Cor. 4:18 NEB). The devastating power of flood, storm, failure of harvest, inflation, economic depression, accident, illness should convince us that some values are not as real as they seem to be. It is not being very smart or practical to build life on the passing material values and sensations which endure at most for a few years and then fade into nothingness. A person whose chief end in life is the amassing of material values will in the end leave nothing but the ashes of a burnt-out life. Only he possesses true wisdom who sets his heart on the eternal values in God. These values are not seen and are therefore not highly appraised by men, but they will show their true and eternal worth when the Lord honors His faithful stewards with His *magna cum laude* citation: "Well done, thou good and faithful servant . . . enter thou into the joy of thy Lord." (Matt. 25:21)

The Momentous Decision

To win us wholeheartedly to the conviction that only permanent values give real and enduring security, and to spare us the remorse of failing to achieve those values, Jesus used strong, compelling language: "If anyone comes to Me and does not hate his own father and mother and wife and children and brothers and sisters, yes, and even his own life, he cannot be My disciple" (Luke 14:26 RSV). These burning words have power to hurl us into the earnest search for their meaning. At first they jar us, as they seem to sweep away all that Jesus taught about family love and the dignity of life. What truth did He want to impart? Certainly He was trying to teach us that our most cherished interests and relationships are to be subordinated to the supreme goal of preserving our life eternally. "What shall it profit a man," He kept on saying, "if he shall gain the whole world and lose his own soul?" (Mark 8:36). Once a person believes in the supreme treasure of life eternal, he will understand why Jesus advised that he sell all that he has in order to buy the field which holds the treasure (Matt. 13:44). It is the desire to experience at last the eternal splendor of life everlasting that will set a man questing for the true security that makes him eternally secure.

Prosperity, Stepping Stone or Stumbling Block?

It is a basic principle of good economics to safeguard and preserve the source of one's wealth. The Holy Spirit constantly directs us to regard God as the Source of wealth and well-being. As this position is challenged by the ways and words of the world, we are obligated to examine the Biblical statements about riches and material possessions.

Jesus did not say that riches will in themselves keep a person out of heaven. It is what riches can do to a person that Jesus is concerned about. Frequently riches put a stumbling block in a man's way to heaven. They often have the effect of making a person proud and conceited. They may, and often do, give a feeling of independence and self-sufficiency. Only a person of resolute purpose, of tough-minded determination, of courageous faith, can resist the momentous power of wealth.

Jesus did not discourage wealth as such. His concern was that His followers should adopt a philosophy that makes wealth a stepping stone instead of a stumbling block. Not money, but the improper love of it, and the subsequent misuse of it, is the root of all evil. Material possessions pose a constant danger to the spiritual life, and they presage ultimate calamity if they are not under the constant control and faithful management of a Christian steward. Jesus commends an economic philosophy which urges the viewing of all property and possessions in terms of functions and obligations rather than in terms of rights and privileges. He does not discourage the normal use of earthly things but proposes their disciplined, sanctified, God-directed use.

"It will be hard for a rich man to enter . . . heaven," Jesus said (Matt. 19:23 RSV). A person who has received large material possessions will find it difficult to accept completely that he is not the creator nor the real owner of his wealth. He will find it even more difficult to come to the honest and consistent conviction that his possessions are tools to be administered in a ministry of love for the good of his fellowmen. The Lord has made His position quite clear. In the day of accounting all those will be honored who took Him at His word and faithfully interpreted His will. Then He will invoke the principle which He revealed to us beforehand, that He cares deeply for the poor and needy: "Inasmuch as ye have done it unto one of the least of these My brethren, ye have done it unto Me." (Matt. 25:40)

Our material standard of living is constantly rising, and with it individual desires are steadily multiplying. With its frozen foods, color television, split-level houses, technology has made possible a standard of living previously unheard of. We are so caught up in the materialistic craze that we hardly know where to stop. The more we have the more we want. *More than enough is no longer enough.* Our ideas of what we ought to have and deserve are constantly growing more fantastic and fictitious.

If we were suddenly reduced to the poverty level of more than a billion people in the world, we would have to get rid of about 90 percent of our furniture, clothing, shoes, and food. We would have to shut off the running water, remove the electric wiring, take away the house itself and move into a glorified toolshed, throw out the bank books, stock certificates, pension plans, cultivate about 3 acres of ground, realize an income of about $300

a year of which a third will go to the landlord and a tenth
to the local moneylender. Above that we would have to
move the nearest clinic or hospital 10 miles away, put
a midwife in charge instead of a doctor, and we would
have to lop off about 20 or 30 years of life expectancy for
every member of the family. That is the ordinary way of life
for about a billion people in our world. If we could truly
put ourselves into the place of these people, we would be
moved to take a new look at the world we are living in. We
might then experience a radical transformation inside ourselves. Perhaps then and only then would our ears be
more sensitive to the cries of rejected humanity in the
world. As a hunger-driven and poverty-ridden humanity
calls out for the church's voice and action, it may be that
the Spirit of God will stir the church to Christlike concern
for the poor and forsaken.

One Light Drives Away Darkness

Every time we hear of the divinely assigned mission
of the church (that's us) to reveal the grace of God for the
healing and salvation of humanity, we are inclined to brush
off our personal obligation with the smug excuse, "I am
only one person, the little I can do would be only a drop
in the bucket." This is the voice of craven escape, not of
courageous attack. Somehow there is enough honesty in
the average Christian to respond appreciatively to the
prayer of the Chinese Christian, "O Lord, reform the
world, beginning with me." Perhaps we all suffer from what
has been diagnosed as "the sin of the saints," a common
affliction which causes a person to demand greater consecration in others while he remains aloof from involvement.
Much of our criticism of the organized church for its failure
to have a more influential voice in the world flows out of
our refusal to demand as much of ourselves as we do of

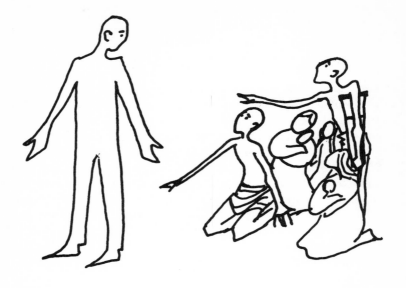

others. The Lord sees through all this sham. There is an inescapable question that demands an answer: *"What would the church be if every person were like me?"* In the great Day of Judgment we will be judged individually, not collectively.

One individual can stir a congregation or community to action. Some believe there is nothing one man or one woman can do against the enormous array of the world's ills. Yet many of the world's achievements have come from the work of a single man. A 33-year-old German monk began the Protestant Reformation, a young Italian explorer discovered the new world, and a young American scientist invented the electric light bulb. Each one of us has the power to exert some influence, however small it may be, for the improvement of some person or group. It is from such diverse acts of faith and courage that human history is shaped. Each time a man stands up for an ideal, defends a principle, says or does something to help others, he becomes a light that drives out darkness.

It takes faith and courage to stand up against the popular position. It is not easy or pleasant to go against the crowd. Even in the church, where the saints get together, it is difficult to be a lone voice for a great and burning cause. Moral courage is a rarer commodity than great intelligence or bravery in battle. Therefore each one of us should live with this reasoning and resolve:

It is true, I am only one, but I am one. I cannot do everything, but I can do something. What I can do I will do, with the help of God.

One night a man took a small candle, lighted it, and began to ascend a long winding staircase. "Where are you going?" asked the candle. "Away high up," said the man. "What are you going to do there?" said the candle. "I am going to show the ships out at sea where the harbor is," said the man, "for we stand here at the entrance to the harbor, and some ships far out on the stormy sea may be looking for our light even now."

"Alas! no ship could ever see my light," said the candle; "it is so very small."

"If your light is small," said the man, "keep burning bright, and leave the rest to me."

When the man got up to the lighthouse, he took the candle and with it lighted the great lamps that stood ready there with their polished reflectors behind them.

You who think your little light of so small account, can you not see what God is able to do with it? Shine and leave the rest to Him.

When Dwight L. Moody heard Henry Varley say, "It remains to be seen what God can do with a person who is totally consecrated to Him," Moody resolved within himself, "By the grace of God I will be that man." It is truly amazing what God is able to do through the witness and example of one consecrated steward in a congregation.

71

Every Christian who has experienced the miraculous mystery of stewardship is bound to be a light that will brighten the path for others.

O Lord, What Is Your Will?

If we want to rise above the poison vapors of materialism into the pure air of freedom to follow God's way, we really have only one way to go. Only the way of stewardship with its recognition of the proper use of wealth can supply the right philosophy in this day of unparalleled material sufficiency, and show us our tremendous potential for good in the world. If this does not happen, if our immense possessions do not give us a consciousness of responsibility and do not lead us to an earnest seeking of God's will to live as God's agents and trustees, the alternative will be enormous growth in conceit, self-sufficiency, arrogance, greed, self-seeking. That will be the beginning of the end, for Christian faith cannot long put up with such strange bedfellows. *There is no man on earth who can accept God's gifts successfully without inquiring about God's will as to their use.* Only the principle of intelligent stewardship can exalt us to the place of properly employing the power God has put into our hands.

If we are sincere in wanting abundant life for ourselves, we should be just as sincere in seeking it for others as well. For us this means setting a Christian standard of living not too high and not too low but definitely where it may still be called Christian. We are not asked to abandon all earthly things. God simply asks us to keep all earthly things under the priority of heavenly concerns. God is asking us to use and manage our earthly possessions in partnership with Him in the interest of living out the meaning of life in terms of love and service. In our voluntary commitment to the stewardship ideal we have the best way to make God's abundant gifts achieve the best things in life for ourselves and others.

There are hundreds of agencies in the world that teach people how to make money and how to amass material possessions. The church is the only agency that is interested in helping us to use and preserve our estate for the good and eternal causes of God. If we could see our total life as it is spread out before God, including its reach into eternity, we would fall on our knees and beg our fellow Christians to keep on instructing and exhorting and guiding us toward a rich and God-honoring stewardship commitment.

5

You *Can* Take It With You

Your Money Is You

Some clever phrases have been used to show how intimately we are linked with our money, "Your money is you"—you are involved in getting it and in using it. "Money is congealed sweat"—it represents your money-producing activity. "Money is crystallized time and talent" —it comes as a result of applying your time, energy, and skill as a salesman, mechanic, builder, teacher, farmer, secretary, truck driver, or any other kind of worker.

The Bible never says that money is evil in itself. We do ourselves and money an injustice when we say that it is evil. By itself it is neither good nor evil; it can, however, be used for either good or evil. Money becomes evil when selfishly hoarded or used to do evil. Money becomes good when used to do good. Under orders of an intelligent steward it has massive power for good. Money can take the wings of the morning to bring the light of the Daystar into the world's dark places; it can bring healing and hope to humanity when used to build hospitals and staff them with doctors and nurses; it can pour handfuls of song and laughter upon orphaned children; it can put warm and loving hands under the physically handicapped who cannot make it on their own; it can spread light and love through churches, seminaries, colleges, schools.

The important thing for us to see clearly is that we are inextricably involved with our money. In using some of it to pay taxes, we are assuming a part in government and public welfare. In using part of it to build and furnish a house, we are providing a home for our dear ones. Through our money we are taking food out of the grocery store and putting it on the table. And when we squander some of it in Las Vegas or at the race track, something of us is lost. *We have a stake, a bit of ourselves, in every cent we earn.*

When the church sends out medical missionaries to rid people of their fear of spirits, to heal them of rickets, scurvy, leprosy, tuberculosis, we ourselves are present in these ministries, for our money is there expressing our love and our concern. Souls won to the eternal kingdom through our stewardship gifts will be eternal trophies of our faith, and Christ will certainly point that out.

The easily forgotten truth that an intimate identification of money with self will extend into eternity becomes luminous in the story of the Chinese Christian who was taunted by an unbelieving neighbor for his resolute adherence to the hope of heaven. "What will you do when you arrive in heaven?" the man asked. In straightforward candor the Chinese Christian answered: "First I will find Christ and I will fall on my knees to thank Him for all He did to redeem me. Next I will walk through the halls of heaven until I find the man who brought me the Gospel by which I was saved." In derisive mockery the unbeliever then asked, "What are you going to do with all your time after that?" His voice ringing with assurance, the humble Christian answered, "After that I hope to find all the people who had a part in sending the man who brought me the Gospel of salvation, and I will bring them to Christ and say to Him, 'These are the people through whose gifts of Christian faith and love I found Your forgiving grace.' "

Money Talks, for Us or Against Us

In one of His many lessons on stewardship Jesus spoke about "unrighteous mammon." Mammon is a Chaldean word meaning riches. Jesus called mammon unrighteous because money is the chief delight and desire of the selfish and unrighteous world which employs much of it for unrighteous purposes. The conscientious Christian tries to use mammon in a righteous manner. This is the course Jesus commends, for He implies no condemnation of property as such. Here are His words: "Make friends for yourselves by means of unrighteous mammon, so that when it fails they may receive you into the eternal habitations" (Luke 16:9 RSV). Jesus is saying that investments in eternal Kingdom causes will themselves become eternal. We will have friends up there who were brought into everlasting habitations through our support of Gospel causes. Long after our money fails to have earthly meaning, the eternal worth of Kingdom investments will endure in the gratitude of those who through them were brought into glory.

Our very best course, therefore, is to invest in the very best cause. The best cause is Christ's cause. The church of Jesus Christ is not only big business; it is everlasting business. The greatest business in the world is the business that Christ paid for on the cross and therefore owns. This business does the greatest amount of good and brings with it the greatest rewards.

"Glory Hole" Economics

When prospectors in California gold rush days discovered a rich gold deposit, they would call it a "glory hole." The Carson Hill glory hole produced a single nugget weighing 195 pounds, valued at $43,530.

The Christian steward discovers his glory hole not in deposits which he takes but in deposits he makes in heavenly work for heavenly treasures. That is what the divine investment broker is saying, "Give, and it will be given to you; good measure, pressed down, shaken together, running over. . . . For the measure you give will be the measure you get back." (Luke 6:38 RSV)

To the business economist who looks at investments only from the earthly point of view this sounds like total nonsense. To God, who is the best investment adviser for the simple reason that He can see the complete returns from every investment, it is pure wisdom. God recommends investments guaranteed for success. The final accounting will prove that not a single investment made on God's advice has failed.

Christians may in full confidence regard God as the best creditor and most trustworthy investment adviser. Their concern need never be that God may not keep His promises. Rather, their concern ought to be that they have the sincere will to follow His advice.

A fully convinced and committed steward will with complete trust accept God's unconditional proposition: "Give, and it will be given to you." This can only mean that we receive by giving rather than by keeping. "Why, that's absurd," the earthling objects, "you will never get ahead that way." "Wrong," says the Lord, "that is the only way you will ever avoid the loss column and get over into the profits column."

How to Preserve Your Estate for Good

God wants to help us preserve our estate for good. Insurance and investment companies propose to help us to a growing estate so long as we live, but no company on earth can promise us an estate we can take with us into the next world. Yet that is precisely what God offers — a valuable estate that will be eternally ours.

Simon Peter employs a banking term when he speaks of an inheritance "reserved in heaven for you" (1 Peter 1:4). This is the inheritance Christ has provided for us. Laboring with Christ and for Him in His redemptive mission, we become His co-workers in building an eternal kingdom. The redemptive causes which we in faith supported are credited to the account of our faith. *Christ made it clear that He will cite our works of love as proofs of faith.* Thus every gift out of a heart sanctified by faith is an investment in the bank that never fails. Even "if anyone gives so much as a cup of cold water to one of these little ones, because he is a disciple . . . that man will assuredly not go unrewarded." (Matt. 10:42 NEB)

In an earthly savings program we are transferring money from our earning years to the years when our earning capacity ceases. Concern for a rainy day is not sinful. God has given the instinct of self-preservation to the squirrel, who stores up food against the winter, and to the human being who makes some provision for the future. So long as it is done within the will of God it is mere common sense to provide for future days on earth. But eyes of faith look beyond earthly horizons to the eternal order of things. God commends the wisdom of using our earthly Kingdom-building years to lay up treasures for the eternal Kingdom years. The teachings of Jesus fairly shout out: "Don't work hard all your life and in the end lose all. Make substantial investments in eternal treasures! Your interest in heavenly causes on earth will produce eternal interest-bearing rewards in heaven."

In the day of *revealing* the Lord will bring to light the good deeds of His children to prove that their faith was genuine and their love true.

Treasures in Heaven

Jesus advised, "Lay up for yourselves treasures in heaven" (Matt. 6:20). What should these words of our Lord mean to us? Doesn't death separate us from earthly treasures? That is what the foolish man in one of the parables of Jesus forgot. He kept on building bigger and bigger barns and surrounding himself with more and more of this world's goods. For that he considered himself very clever. But Jesus said he was a fool. He certainly was not a fool in resourcefulness, for he knew how to increase his earthly estate. Jesus labeled him a fool because he was not smart enough to preserve his possessions beyond this world. This is the tragedy reenacted over and over again in our day. Leaving God out, a man may work hard all his life and in the end have neither God nor eternal dividends from his estate. One can detect a mood of sadness in Jesus' words: "Then whose shall these things be?" Everything the man had gained by hard work was irretrievably lost.

He lost not only his possessions but himself as well. The man took nothing with him into the other world except a record of unbelief and unfaithfulness. Muffing his opportunity to prosper by going God's way, he chose to go his own way and he lost. Jesus wrote his epitaph: "Here lies a fool." Men may have thought him the richest man in the cemetery, but according to God's rating he was a pauper. (Luke 12:16-20)

Jesus applies the lesson of the story to us: "So is he that layeth up treasure for himself and is not rich toward God." (Luke 12:21)

Never Good-bye Forever

Christians never say good-bye for the last time. They know they will meet each other again, if not in this world then in the next.

The parallel applies to our investments in God's kingdom. Sometimes we experience the fruitage of such investments in earthly blessings, but the eternal blessings are unquestionably greater. Kingdom investments are the only ones we shall never lose. Someday we will be separated from our stocks and bonds, cars and houses, lands and jewels, and all other earthly values, but we will never be separated from the eternal benefits of investments in God's eternal causes. Treasures laid up in heaven are not subject to theft, fire, inflation, or any other erosive force.

Once there is a breakthrough to this point of view it will no longer be necessary for the church to cajole unwilling gifts from people who secretly resist and resent giving. No longer will they associate giving with something unpleasant, like pulling teeth. Christian investments will no longer be made in the "good-bye forever" mood. Christians will no longer need to say or think, when they make investments in God's bank, "Well that is one investment I will never see again," for they know that the very opposite is true. *These are the only investments we shall ever see again.* When people are convinced that there really is no other way in which to preserve their estate for good, they will give with a new feeling of purpose and meaning. They will see the good sense of taking from an estate which they cannot keep for investments in one which they cannot lose.

Not One World but Two

God has made us citizens of two worlds, and He wants us to be good citizens of both and to inherit the best blessings of both. To live it up in this world without regard to the coming world is in fact a denial of the truth that our life extends into eternity. Investment counselors say that it is foolish to put all your eggs into one basket. They advise a diversification of investments. Should one fail, another may succeed. Our investment portfolio should show a good balance of investments for earthly gain and for heavenly gain. The heart of the matter is to fit every act of life into the scheme of eternal values. Thus every act of stewardship while we are on this earth becomes an entry in the page of eternity.

What About Rewards?

We do not become good stewards or practice good stewardship because we have our eyes on rewards. Rewards are not the motive, but they certainly will be the result of stewardship faithfulness. God has made this unmistakably clear.

One day Simon Peter, presuming to speak for the Twelve, who perhaps had been discussing the point, confronted Jesus with the question of rewards: "We have left everything and followed You. What then shall we have?" Jesus said to them, "Everyone who has left houses or brothers or sisters or father or mother or children or lands, for My . . . sake, will receive a hundredfold, and inherit eternal life." (Matt. 19:27, 29 RSV)

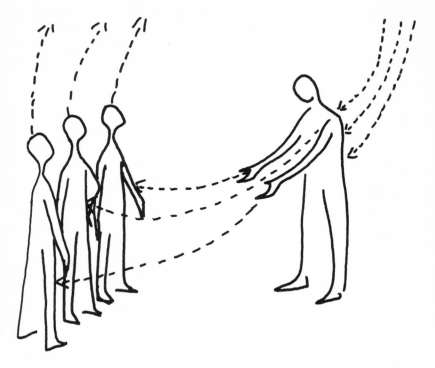

One might have expected Jesus to brush aside Peter's question with a sharp rebuke, "Shame on you, Peter, for even thinking of rewards. Am I not a sufficient reward for your efforts in My behalf?" But Jesus did not in any wise rebuke the disciples. Instead, He answered their question in a manner which leaves no room for doubts about lavish rewards.

It would be an absurd conclusion to think that the rewards of the new world will literally bring a 100 for 1 return on every Kingdom investment, but it would also be a base and inglorious judgment to disclaim or downgrade our Lord's promise. That He promises a "hundredfold" reward plus an inheritance of eternal life to His true followers cannot be disputed. Yet, talk of rewards is hushed up by some as though it were suspect and quite beyond the sphere of moral virtue. When the question of rewards comes up, stewardship leaders begin to pussyfoot as though they were walking on eggs. Perhaps it is the fear of crossing the line between grace and works that makes them so fearful and cautious. The concern to preserve the integrity of divine grace is virtuous, but God does not seem to go along with us in our conclusion that grace rules out rewards. *God hasn't been afraid to offer rewards even beyond our understanding.* He has done it all through His Word. Not only has He promised rich rewards, but He has dared us to test His promises of reward: "Bring ye all the tithes into the storehouse . . . and prove Me now herewith, saith the Lord of hosts, if I will not open unto you the windows of heaven and pour you out a blessing that there shall not be room enough to receive it." (Mal. 3:10)

Rewards may not always be in money or material goods, but will always be in what is best for us. They may not always come at once, but they will come at the right time. And they will be rewards of divine grace. After all, our work for God is nothing more or less than His work in us. Even our response to His grace is grace pure and simple. All we can say about His promised rewards of grace upon our faithful stewardship is that this is grace upon grace.

6

Questing for the Miracle

The Firstfruits Withholding Plan

Workers in the United States have become accustomed to the wage withholding plan. They may not like it, but they accept it for the common good. They know that only a rigid plan will guarantee fixed and constant support of the vast government complex of public services. In spite of their protests against increasing taxation, most citizens realize that their own economic stability is interlocked with that of the government. Some noble souls with a deep concern for the public weal pay taxes cheerfully, even thankfully. In the government's claim of a substantial share of their income they see the public concern for the poor, the aged, the sick, the blind, and many other people and causes. Deep in their hearts they are happy over their share in social welfare.

If the withholding plan works out well in the earthly kingdom, ought it not work out as well in God's kingdom? The very fact that God is the originator of the idea gives it plausible merit. In the Old Testament the withholding plan was legally mandatory. Kingdom citizens who evaded the withholding principle by refusing the tithe were held in contempt of God. "Robbers of God," the prophet Malachi called them, 3:8.

The New Testament retains the withholding principle. "Upon the first day of the week let every one of you lay by him in store as God hath prospered him" (1 Cor. 16:2). Higher motivation on the higher ground of grace has shifted the principle from the duty level to the love and privilege level. The "have to" pressure has given way to the "want to" privilege. The lover of God is glad to have a vital share in the advancement of the Kingdom. Free from the tithe tax, he now voluntarily taxes himself as God requires.

By our acceptance or rejection of the voluntary withholding of God's share, we place ourselves on record. We show whether we believe in and accept God's way or not. It is up to us now. We can cheat if we want to, but we will only be cheating ourselves. Aware of it or not, we are taking a stand for or against God's plan. Our answer is "yes" or "no." By our "yes" answer we are saying that we are vitally involved in Kingdom affairs, interested in Kingdom growth, desirous of Kingdom blessings and Kingdom honors. By our "no" answer we are saying that we are not much impressed with the honor or the demands of discipleship as shown in Jesus' words, "You are My friends if you do what I command you. . . . I have called you friends." (John 15:14-15)

As God Prospers

The one explicit New Testament principle of giving is the *firstfruits withholding* principle. This is the plan God Himself has laid down. No plan devised by man can match this one for effectiveness. It has everything a good plan ought to have. It is faith-oriented, practical, intelligent, workable, rewarding. Being God's plan, it has pure virtue. *The person who has the interest of the church at heart will at once see in it the good sense which commends acceptance.* Coming straight from the heart of God, the plan goes straight into the heart of a straightforward child of God. There is no other known plan that will insure the steady flow of Kingdom support.

God's plan is precise and simple. It leaves us with one single and solemn responsibility, *to give to God as God gives to us.* Our giving now is determined by the constancy of God's gifts to us. If God gives us much, then we give Him proportionately much; if God gives us little, then we give Him proportionately little. Giving to the Lord no longer rests on arbitrary caprice or on momentary moods. *It is as constant as the Giver's gifts and the believer's thankful response to those gifts.*

God's share is to be withheld out of God's gifts before anything is set aside for personal use. Whether it be the check for weekly wages or a dividend check on stocks, or the profit from a real estate sale, or an inheritance gift, God's share is set aside first. That is the deliberate choice of the dedicated steward who has decided to be faithful to God's ordinance. The government has already withheld its share from our wages or our inheritance. Here we had no choice. But when it comes to withholding God's share, the choice is ours. If our conscience is sensitive to God's will, and if we extend our thinking to the edge of eternity, if we want our lives to count for the Kingdom, and if we desire eternal investments, we will do what is best all around, we will give God His share cheerfully, faithfully, consistently.

The *firstfruits withholding* plan is God's method for the undergirding of the vast ministries of the Gospel with financial support. God's way is the only way we can imagine through which He can increase the outflow of gifts for Gospel work. *If the outflow is always kept in proportion to the inflow, then God can provide the funds needed for Gospel expansion.* Otherwise He cannot—at least we know of no other way in which He chooses to do it. A person who remains true to the *firstfruits withholding* principle whenever God increases His gifts to him will faithfully acknowledge God's generosity by increasing his gifts in ratio to the increase God has granted. On the other hand, a person who keeps God's share for himself is unwittingly tying God's hands as far as he himself and his Kingdom involvement is concerned.

There are at least two factors in modern life which point up the need of God's *firstfruits withholding* principle:

First, there is the mobility of the American people, which is expected to go on expanding. Forty million Americans move every year. Many of these are church members severing their ties with a hometown congregation. Now it is obvious that if the giving-drive of these people has been only parochially oriented and motivated by the support of the home parish and not by God's principle of *firstfruits withholding*, there will be a twofold loss: the loss by the individual of God's blessings and of Kingdom investments, and the loss by the church of substantial revenue. For their walk within the will of God, for their steady investments in the eternal Kingdom, Christians should be as constant in the practice of their *firstfruits withholding* as in their worship. Whether at home or on the move, they are to be instant and constant in their worship of God by praying, praising, thanking, and giving. Neither the individual member nor the church can afford the loss that results from irregular, capricious, arbitrary giving. Faithful, wholehearted compliance with God's *firstfruits withholding* plan is the route for the intelligent, responsible steward.

A second factor pointing up the critical need for the adoption of the *firstfruits withholding* principle is *the radical change in the established church structure.* Fifty years ago the average church got along with a simple organizational setup. Its full-time staff consisted only of the pastor. The organist, choir leader, sexton were usually part-time employees. Denominational headquarters and local administrative offices were tended by a small crew of full-time workers. But things are different now. Denominational headquarters are staffed with hundreds of workers, and the various ministries are headed by trained specialists. Many single churches have a staff of 5 to 20 full-time workers. In this respect the churches are keeping in step with the federal, state, county, and city governments with their ever-increasing number of boards, bureaus, agencies, supervisors, inspectors, and secretaries. Demands for the increase of public services call for the increase of public servants. Each such increase adds to the public tax burden. This process will not only continue but expand. It's the principle of "supply and demand" — supplying the demand for expanded services.

The same trend is developing in the churches. As their ministries expand, they see the need for highly trained specialists to help people in their marital, social, psychological problems. Extended ministries require expanded financial support. The church will not long lay effective claim on the loyalty of professional workers who are conspicuously underpaid.

Putting these factors together, it becomes obvious that an entirely new set of stewardship standards is needed. Yesterday's standards are not adequate for today's needs.

What is the answer to the problem? There is only one completely right and true answer. It is the adoption on the part of all Christians of God's *firstfruits withholding* principle. Nothing less than that will do. Nor will anything other than that. Once the church has won its members to see the intelligence, the soundness, and the workability of this plan, it must resolutely abandon all other plans in conflict with it. It will be a case of going God's way and succeeding or going man's way and failing.

God's plan will work! The very fact that it is His supports that conviction. Even chronically faultfinding church members will be unable to detect a flaw in the plan which God has provided. *People will respond to God's plan if it is properly explained and understood.* One can usually count on church people being loyal to what they respect and respecting what obviously does good and helps people. Because they see the simple honesty in God's plan, its limitless potential for good, the vastly increased church support which it engenders, the generous blessings that will follow, Christian people will adopt it. One may assume without fear of contradiction that the average Christian is too honest to turn it down. But if the churches are sincere in recommending God's plan, they will have to practice what they preach. To recommend God's plan one day and to deny it the next, by espousing money-raising campaigns which imply a tacit denial of God's plan, will never do. If the churches cannot with full trust in the success of God's plan promise their members that there will be no deviation from it once they have adopted it as their own, their small-ness of faith and lack of integrity will invite a correspondingly lame response.

The pledge and promise of church members that they will practice the *firstfruits withholding* plan is the only one the church can in good conscience exact from them. No responsible and sincere church can in good conscience demand a precise and stated pledge of a certain amount of money. People are afraid of a pledge like that, and therefore they shy away from it or keep it as low as possible to play it safe. Only God's plan is good enough to safeguard the church's financial stability.

From the Top Always

The genius of God's principle, which must not be violated, is that God's share is given from the top, not from the bottom. Scraping the bottom for God brings Him dregs and brings the giver regret. Giving God the first sanctifies the rest. *How can God be in all of it when His share comes from the bottom?* The blessings are always from the top down, not from the bottom up. This is to be a venture of faith, not of doubt. Yet there is always an element of doubt when a person is required to make a precise, stated money pledge, for a person does not even know if he will live through the year or if he will retain his employment and his health. However, a Christian will not hesitate to make a pledge which he is sure he can keep. And he can keep the kind that asks him to give only in proportion to God's gifts, with a promise to take God's share from the top.

We are sailing too close to the shore if we wait to see how we fare before we give God His share. Faith is demonstrated when we launch out into the deep, believing from the heart that God knows our promise and intent and that He will certainly not allow a man to have less for his needs because he has first honored the Giver. This is not tempting God or testing Him. It is simply trusting Him. No man lifting his faith to God will be let down by God. It has been demonstrated time after time that a man will not "come behind in any gift" (1 Cor. 1:7) because he gave God His share first. When we give God His share first, we show that we trust Him first, love Him first, and need Him first.

Too Idealistic? Never!

Why should it be so difficult to get this idea across to people who have seen God's love shining from the cross? The advocates of puny and impotent man-made programs cry themselves hoarse: "It will never work." "The plan is too idealistic." "Our way is better." Wrong! This is the only plan that will work. It will work because it comes from God and will be under His blessing.

There is proof galore that man's various proposals have been found wanting. For example, the wave of resentment against the church for its constant cry for cash! We have evidence enough that man-made methods have failed. What we need is enough honesty to admit it! Aggregate funds received by any denomination may appear very great, but farseeing church members know that they are inadequate. What the churches are doing is a mere drop in the bucket compared to what is needed. The truth is we are not getting the job done fast enough. The one commodity that gives life and light and hope and joy and peace to people through Christ's redemptive work is not getting around. And the reason for our failure is always the same: "No money!" So we keep on pleading and pounding, but the results do not vary. Giving is not increasing with the growing population, the growing economy, and the growing inflation. Everybody is bemoaning deficits, resenting the frequent money appeals, and the churches are facing the discord and divisiveness which money problems beget. If this teaches us anything, it should show us that man's way is a total flop.

"O Ye of Little Faith"

Why should there be reluctance to switch over to God's way? In secular business, men are sharp enough to look for better methods toward greater efficiency. God's plan is potentially so limitless, so promising of good, it is so simple and sincere, so honest and intelligent, that one would expect every Christian to rush toward it. But the opposite seems true. Even church leaders, who should know better, hedge and hesitate, express fears and doubts, and show little enthusiasm for the plan. Many pastors want none of it. Church boards frown on it. So the diamond is thrown away with the broken glass. Why? There can be only one answer. It is fear. Church leaders fear an even greater crash in the church coffers. They are scared to death that God's plan will mean the end of any hope for fiscal prosperity in the church. They feel much more comfortable and secure with a plan in their hands instead of a plan in the hands of God. It is amazing that people can hypnotize themselves to feel so comfortable with failure that they are afraid of success.

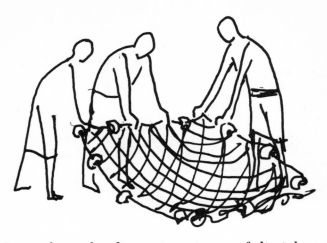

So we have the distressing picture of disciples who have labored all night and caught nothing but who are unwilling to cast out their net for the great haul that awaits them under God's promise. *It is sad beyond words that people who trust God for salvation are unwilling to trust Him for anything else, gifts far inferior to the salvation gift.* Perhaps we need to see that fear and faith cancel each other out. Someone has said that the Bible says, "Fear not" 365 times—one "Fear not" for every day of the year. The oft-repeated words of Jesus, "Fear not; only believe" will be a great help to the person wrestling with the question, "Shall I, or shall I not, adopt God's *firstfruits withholding* plan for my life?" No one need ever fear going God's way in faith. It is going the other way in unbelief that we need to fear.

Plans and Safeguards

When the church is alive to its task and aware of its divine mission, it will offer its children many opportunities for the investment of their talents, time, and treasures. Those who want to be ready to make their investments when the opportunity beckons will have to lay their plans and provide some safeguards against failure. To seize the opportunity for a God-pleasing investment of our funds, we may make use of the practice which some serious Christians have adopted:

The Lord's Treasury

Most Christians who follow the *firstfruits withholding* plan will not encounter much of a problem either in computing the Lord's share or in finding the best way to give it back to Him. There are, however, definite dangers lurking in the shadows. Is the Lord's percentage to be computed on the basis of gross or net income? When and how shall the Lord's share be returned to Him? The temptation is always there to borrow from the Lord's share or to delay setting it aside. To head off a number of potential problems, some Christians provide a depository or container of some kind which they think of as the Lord's treasury. Whenever they realize income of any kind, they take the Lord's firstfruits from the top and place that percentage into the treasury, keeping the Lord's money separate from other funds. Thus it is always ready and intact. When the time comes to place the Lord's funds, either through the local church or some other agency, their giving will not be done "grudgingly or of necessity," but cheerfully. A person will be happy to have on hand funds which have already been dedicated to the Lord and are now disbursed as opportunities invite or an adopted program directs.

The Opportunity Pile

The Holy Spirit has told us to be ready, "as we have opportunity to do good to all men, especially to those who are of the household of faith" (Gal. 6:10). Every Christian will give ready assent to the observation that a person is almost deluged with appeals for donations in support of all kinds of causes. One Christian with whom we discussed this aspect of life in the United States produced a batch of 34 separate appeals that had come to him through the mails in a single month. Perhaps most of these appeals are good and worthy. The least worthy are those that presume our support by mailing us merchandise which may either be kept and paid for or returned if not wanted, usually at our expense. Though one dislikes to be taken in by unscrupulous people or methods, the fact remains that there are many causes which commend our support. All such appeals may be placed on what some Christians have called an "opportunity pile." Then, as the opportunity arises, we may do as much as we can. It is an exciting hill to climb. By combining the plan of the Lord's treasury and of the opportunity pile, we shall give ourselves the joyful satisfaction of being ready to make investments for worthy causes that put a strong claim upon our Christian spirit and conduct.

Shall We Make a Pledge?

Sometimes one wonders where the idea of making a pledge to support God's work originated. Did it come out of the desire of Christians to safeguard their decisions against lapses and corresponding losses or did it come from church boards which demanded a pledge of support before promoting church programs and projects? The idea behind the practice of the pledge certainly has its corollary in the many pledges God has made to us. God, who always stands by His word, has put His repeated pledges into writing in His inspired Scriptures. Here are a few of them:

He pledged us a Savior (Matt. 1:21; John 3:16). He pledged us the Holy Spirit to guide us (John 14:26). He pledged us "new heavens and a new earth" (2 Peter 3:13). He pledged us "an overflowing blessing" for faithfulness in stewardship. (Mal. 3:10-12)

Some Christians ask why they should make a pledge in writing when they have already made a decision in their minds to return to the Lord a certain percentage of His granted gifts. To be sure, there is no commandment in the Bible or rule of the church that makes the pledge mandatory. Why then make a pledge? Pledging is in the tradition and spirit of many examples given in the Bible of faithful and true children of God who entered a specific covenant with the Lord, often in a dramatic form like Jacob's pledge to tithe (Gen. 28:22) or St. Paul's pledge to keep a vow (Acts 18:18). Moreover, making a pledge will lead us to more careful and earnest thought and preparation: Our pledge will show (1) that we recognize God's ownership of everything, (2) that we trust His wisdom and love to give us all things needful without waiting to see how much we will get before saying what we will share, (3) that we love God more than the things of this world, (4) that we know His eternal gift will never be equaled by our fruit-bearing, (5) that we ask His help and blessing upon our resolve to be a true and faithful steward, (6) that we desire to set up a safeguard against the love of money overcoming our love of God.

Purpose of the Church Budget

The church budget does not provide a proper motive for giving. It merely presents a cost appraisal of the church's Christian work program. The budget is a distribution plan for money as received, not a promotional tool to encourage increased giving. It shows that there has been careful and businesslike planning for Christian service locally and in the world outreach. Church members will take a much more intelligent and sympathetic view of the budget if they have a share in composing it. The budget is to be democratically arrived at. If all are expected to uphold by their time, talents, and treasures the work program as represented in the budget, it is no more than right that all have a voice in deciding what the program should be. By giving every member the opportunity of suggesting items to be added to or deleted from the budget, people will proudly claim it as "our" budget rather than disdainfully reject it as "their" budget.

One of the worst things to do with the budget is to divide its total cost by the total membership, then suggest that each member assume an equal share of its support. The unintelligent and unspiritual idea that the budget is to suggest the average of each member's fair share is as injurious to the true stewardship life as sand in the motor. Sound stewardship ideas will never thrive in that kind of atmosphere.

The Unified Budget

Congregations that wish to be wholehearted and consistent in preserving the integrity of the stewardship way will lay plans for the eventual elimination of all special offerings. This is best achieved by the use of a fully unified budget which covers all the causes entitled to financial support, local and denominational. A fully unified budget provides subsidy for all the organizations and societies that are doing the work of the church and are therefore entitled to its support. The unified budget includes denominational programs and projects. The only way to head off special offerings is to anticipate them and include them in the budget, whether they are under congregational or denominational auspices. If church leaders have not planned their work well enough to allow advance notice to the local budget makers, then it is doubtful that these programs merit support. One must, of course, allow the possibility of natural catastrophes or acts of God which may arise unexpectedly and place a claim of compassionate response upon the conscience of a congregation.

The importance of ruling out special offerings and money campaigns can hardly be overemphasized. These always weaken the stewardship process. In their very nature they aim to make the most of the moment and the least of retaining and protecting the steady flow of gifts over the long haul. This conviction may justifiably direct congregations to notify denominational headquarters that they will gladly and generously support all synodical programs which can be included in the local budget, but they will disclaim responsibility for supporting an arbitrary, unannounced, and unbudgeted money campaign which catches them by surprise. Since such an action represents a new position, congregations may have to put up with the idea of special denominational offerings for some years. However, with the growth of true stewardship ideals, these can be at first restricted and then entirely eliminated. This suggestion may have the immediate effect of stirring up the viewers-with-alarm. But there is no real reason for that kind of disturbance. If it is God's way that we are proposing, there is nothing to fear, for God's way cannot fail.

Obviously, congregations must practice at home what they are preaching to their denominations. Members who have pledged themselves to the *firstfruits withholding* plan should be assured that there will be no special appeals of any kind. And if the members are expected to be constant in their giving, they can expect their congregation to be just as constant in the administration of the gifts. The arbitrary, seasonal, impulsive element is to be overcome both in giving and in administering the gifts. When both the congregation and the denomination consistently honor and practice this policy, there will be no trouble at all. To allow for contingencies from unforeseen and unpreventable emergencies such as natural disasters, the church may provide a few extra envelopes which a member may use, if desired, for gifts over and above the regular percentage decided upon. By providing from six to ten plain, numbered envelopes, included in the regular carton, a church honors the right of a member to give to any cause over and above the budget with the understanding that the church will so honor the gift. This is about the only way a person can give additional funds for a cause through his church and its records. This method also provides a convenient way for a member to give to a cause not included in the church budget.

The Last Will and Testament

A person's last will is the last word he has to say about the estate God has entrusted to his hands. While we are alive it is within our power to distribute our estate as we will. *After death, however, it is too late to assert our will.* Perhaps nothing will speak to our children so effectively about our faith as the designation of an honorable share of our estate for godly causes in recognition of God's grace and generosity. There is no Scriptural principle which can be invoked to require a man who has been a faithful and good steward all his life to designate additional funds for the Lord's cause in his last will and testament. If he has practiced *firstfruits withholding* and has given an honorable percentage of the Lord's gifts for the Lord's causes, then all that is left of his estate is certainly under the aura and blessing of Christian consecration. The remembrance

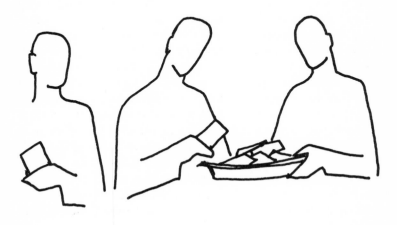

of the Lord's cause in the last will is a bonus, an additional proof of our desire to make our estate count for Him. In this way the estate that remains for final distribution to children is doubly sanctified, by the *firstfruits withholding* practice and by an additional act of stewardship in dedicating a second share to the Lord. It may be remembered, however, that in many cases people have not begun practicing percentage giving until later in life. In such a case the decision to set aside the Lord's share in the will is merely a delayed payment of long overdue firstfruits.

The Sealed Pledge

Before this manuscript went to press, it was read by a number of people who are known to be good stewards. Each one of these expressed disapproval of any publication of members' contributions. This practice, it was held, may lead to uncharitable and impious judgments which engender gossip. When a member's contribution appears to be on the generous side, the person appraising it is tempted to injurious conclusions, disparaging the liberal giver: "He must have discovered a gold mine." "With all his holdings and investments, he should be giving a lot more." Small donations evoke equally damaging comments: "No wonder he can't give more, with all his trips, new cars, indulgent spending." "You'd think they would be ashamed to hide behind a puny contribution like that, expecting others to pay their share." The publication of people's gifts for public consumption is a legalistic device which ought to be thoroughly renounced and permanently repudiated. For all the pride it has encouraged and the shame it has wrought, the plan deserves to be killed and buried somewhere in a nameless grave on boot hill.

Similar denunciation was voiced against the use of an open pledge card with a definite dollar sum pledged. The pretense that the church program for the coming year could not be planned properly unless officials could add up the pledges and see how much money is available was held untenable. Every business firm in the country operates with a budget based on estimated income. Even the most efficient computer, using the best available information from charts, graphs, and past-performance records, cannot with certainty and precision predict the economic status of the nation a year in advance. Moreover, the church should realize that it is quite impossible for a member who practices percentage giving to know the precise amount of his giving for the year.

It was the consensus of stewards whose opinion was solicited that the Sealed Pledge method is most in harmony with true and pure stewardship principles. In a covenant between himself and his God the steward writes down *what percentage of the Giver's gifts he plans to return to Him.* The envelope which holds the solemn agreement is sealed and brought to the Lord's altar, where it remains throughout the year as a silent yet eloquent token of the faith and love of the steward. At the end of the year it is returned to the member with seal unbroken. Because this covenant is secret, it is sealed and remains sealed as long as it is not in the possession of the pledger.

The Sealed Pledge is not a new device to raise money. There is no motivating power in it. Some congregations, assuming that it will, of itself, accomplish wonders, have been disappointed with it. Expecting the mechanics of a plan to accomplish a sudden turnabout in the attitudes and convictions of people is like expecting a watchcase without the inner works to keep time. The Sealed Pledge is only a small part of a plan to win people to Scriptural stewardship convictions. Its strength lies in its endeavor to bring people into a direct encounter with the Lord in making their stewardship decisions. It attempts to encourage a sincere dialog between the steward who loves the Lord and the Lord who loves the steward. The essential purpose of that get-together is to achieve a meeting of the mind and will, pleasing alike to God and to God's steward-servant. Obviously the Sealed Pledge cannot accomplish this kind of rapport; it merely encourages and accommodates it.

Why a Secret Pledge?

The very nature of the transaction between the steward and his Lord is secret in character. *The relationship between a man and his God is personal and intimate.* The first step in making the pledge is a step toward God in prayer, asking for His help. The second step, too, is secret and personal, for each one must act for himself and make his own decision in the pledge. Both these steps are in harmony with the Lord's own words: "When thou prayest, enter into thy closet, and when thou hast shut thy door, pray to thy Father which is in secret . . . that thine alms may be in secret; and thy Father, which seeth in secret, Himself shall reward thee openly" (Matt. 6:6, 4). There is, nevertheless, an element of public testimony in the Sealed Pledge plan. The sealed envelope, placed by the steward on the Lord's altar, dedicated there together with the pledges of other members, remains at the altar through the year to bear public witness of participation in this sincere and God-honoring plan.

The Sealed Pledge, which grew out of the stewardship revival movement in Faith Lutheran Church, Los Angeles and Inglewood, Calif., has had an enigmatic career. Its friends cannot say enough for it; its enemies cannot cease speaking against it. We are confident that those who have been disappointed in their trial-flight experiment with the Sealed Pledge used it in a manner that invited failure. At the time of its inception we said this about the plan: "The Sealed Pledge is not a new plan or a new device to raise money. It is, in itself, not a plan at all, and it is certainly not a substitute for a spiritually based, Christ-centered stewardship program. Used as a part of a sound stewardship program, the Sealed Pledge simply dramatizes and visualizes the secret covenant between the bountiful Giver and the faithful steward-servant."

What the opponents do not like about the Sealed Pledge is its secret element. Somehow they feel that this is downright dangerous. Why, a man can get by with anything that way. You just don't feel safe letting people play around with liberty like that. They'll turn it into license every time.

So these people with little faith and big fear propose that, to keep people on their toes, there will have to be an open pledge for human eyes to see and human judgment to approve. But these fearful men will have to admit that they cannot consistently practice the principle they espouse. We would like to ask them: If, as they suggest, the church derives such undoubted benefits from the fanfare of sounding trumpets when something is done for the Lord, why limit the publicity to money gifts? If we like this business of trumpet sounding, which Jesus explicitly denounced, why not publicize all the love-acts of Christian people, the number of times they have served and forgiven each other, their visits to the sick, their private prayers, and their church and Communion attendance? If publicity is so important, why not publicize the higher graces? It doesn't speak well for us when we become most excited from seeing the one flash of the many-faceted diamond of stewardship that involves money. One has the feeling that more flares of enthusiasm would go up in some churches over the announcement of a million dollar gift than of the conversion to Christ of a dozen souls.

A Tree for Fruit-bearing or Hiding?

Churches may fear that members will enthusiastically vote in the Sealed Pledge and vote out all money campaigns and special offerings only to evade their responsibilities even more. They will soon turn their new liberties into license. Civil disobedience and lawlessness in the United States give proof that citizens will use up and abuse their liberties without the slightest feeling of responsibility to contribute anything to their preservation and promotion. Thus license becomes the curse of liberty. Will this happen in the church when the stewardship life gets out of the hands of man and is fully abandoned to the hands of God? Doesn't the Sealed Pledge plan totally remove the possibility of checking up on the members' giving and of disciplining the delinquent? Does not this system allow people, if they so choose, to do next to nothing without anyone but God knowing about it? Yes, it is true. *The Sealed Pledge plan provides a bush behind which people may conveniently hide, if that is what they want.* It is to be remembered, however, that in the church of Jesus Christ we are in the major league, not in the bush league. What may happen is more than offset by what will happen when a church adopts a fully God-honoring stewardship system. It may give some people a more convenient excuse to evade their responsibilities, but that should not bother us too much; the person who wants excuses will always find more than he can use.

Unspiritual people often join the visible church and make their influence felt within it. But the consecrated majority, united in the greatest cause and for the best purpose in the world, will in the end prevail. There is a verse in the Bible which is called the Martyr's Motto: "He that is unjust, let him be unjust still; and he which is filthy, let him be filthy still; and he that is righteous, let him be righteous still; and he that is holy, let him be holy still" (Rev. 22:11). These words simply say: "If you insist on being a wanton and worldly person, if that is what you want, then go ahead and choose that, but consider that you will die as you live and you will be judged as you die."

In the church you can't force people one way or another. It is best just to be transparently honest and tell people that this stewardship plan will help them to become like trees of the Lord's planting, richly laden with fruit unto life everlasting, or it will offer them trees of escape behind which they may hide from their fellow Christians for a season but which will not hide them from the eyes of God forever.

Light for the Path Ahead

Only through faithful stewardship does the society of the redeemed become the society of the concerned. As science and automation open up new vistas of opportunity for man, it is important for Christian leaders to bring the light of God's Word to the path on which future generations will walk. The divine stewardship principle is linked to Christian faith. It is as constant as faith, and will not vary with changing economic conditions. If the future medium of exchange shifts to credit cards and the use of automated devices for a cashless economy, the Christian's stewardship life will remain constant. Loyalty to Christ will find a way of expressing itself in spite of the shifting moods and practices of contemporary economics.

Economic forecasters say that poverty will for the most part be abolished in the United States. Within a few years more than half of all income, they say, will be available for discretionary spending, not obligatory as are payments for rent or food. Products formerly considered luxuries will be regarded as necessities. There will be a boom in luxury fads like boats, sport cars, private planes. Perhaps our biggest stewardship problem and opportunity will be the fact that $10 billion or more will be in the hands of young people, most of whom will continue to have superficial values until they catch the vision of the glory and beauty of life as a partnership with the Lord Jesus Christ.

What Percentage Shall We Pledge?

The New Testament does not offer an explicit answer to the question: "What percentage of the Giver's gifts shall be used for the cause nearest the Giver's heart?" Nor does it tell us whether to figure the percentage from the gross or the net income. *Somehow our Christian faith and love must provide the answer.* Every Christian should adopt a principle which he thinks is right and God-pleasing. Only he can decide on what to base the percentage and what the percentage itself should be. Some good stewards feel that it is easier and better to give a percentage of gross income, even if this should mean lowering the percentage. Others, specifically businessmen who obviously could not base their giving on gross income, operate with net income as their percentage base. One church has worked out this solution, which seems to have enjoyed ready response: Members give 8% of their gross income, plus 1% on each additional $25 income above a weekly salary of $150, less 1% for each dependent child. Whatever

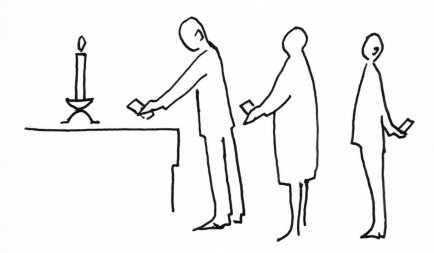

our decision, God will know what it is and how we arrived at it. The important step is to get started with percentage giving and to continue with it religiously. The personal satisfaction and happiness found in pursuing this policy usually leads to the desire and decision to increase the percentage from year to year, as God increases faith and love and gives proof that His blessings are "exceeding abundantly above all that we ask or think." (Eph. 3:20)

The only guideline God has laid down for New Testament Christians is that they give in proportion to His gifts. We are free to make our own decision within the framework of that instruction. The irksome bondage of Old Testament demands is past. We are under the guidance of the Holy Spirit, the compulsion of Christian love, and the obligation to be true to the joyful relationship that exists between ourselves and our God through the Lord Jesus Christ. In addition to the direction to keep our giving in proportion to His, God did say that "Each one must do as he has made up his mind, not reluctantly or under compulsion, for God loves a cheerful giver" (2 Cor. 9:7 RSV). Another Scripture affirms that our deciding and giving should be done in the climate of a "willing mind." (2 Cor. 8:12)

God has put us on our own on the ground of being His own. This makes our choice more delightful but also more difficult. It would require much less effort on our part if God had placed New Testament Christians under the law of the tithe. We have to admit, of course, that a law like that would be out of harmony with the delightful freedoms we now enjoy. In the light of these freedoms we want our decision to be candidly honest, pleasing to God, the kind we can live with in good conscience, representing the very best choice we can possibly make as children of the new life and the new liberty.

As pointed out in an earlier chapter, no one should even attempt to make the choice for us, for God wants the choice to be ours. It is to be the expression of our faith, our love, our gratitude, and our trust in God's promises.

Shall It Be the Tithe?

That the giving of the tithe was a command for Old Testament believers no one will deny; that it is a command for New Testament Christians few will affirm. The important question for New Testament Christians is this: Is the principle of the tithe worthy of serious consideration? We may contend with justification that the giving of the tithe as the Lord's share is fully as deserving of acceptance as is the giving of one day in seven for public divine worship. *Neither the tithe law nor the Sabbath law are binding on New Testament Christians.* The Holy Spirit has made it abundantly clear that they stand on the higher ground of grace. For them the question is: Should the ceiling be lowered or raised because they are on higher ground? Should the Lord's share be below the tithe, exactly on the level of the tithe, or beyond the tithe?

There seems to be something curiously inconsistent about accepting the Lord's Day principle, which is patterned after the Old Testament Sabbath law, and rejecting the tithe principle, which is patterned after the Old Testament 10-percent-withholding law. We readily abandon the tithe principle on the ground that it does not apply to the New Testament Christians, but we insist on retaining the Old Testament Sabbath principle, which is just as little binding on them. We are guilty of a strange inconsistency in coming to such radically different conclusions with regard to these two Old Testament laws. We don't hesitate to remind a member who is remiss in his Sunday church attendance that every conscientious Christian should operate with the rule never to bypass the Sunday divine service for light reasons. We grow eloquent about the glory and beauty of the Lord's Day as the very beginning of the eternal rest which God has promised to His beloved children. All this is right and good. But what do we say about the Old Testament tithe? Should we not say with impartial vigor that Christians living under grace are as freely motivated to honor God's principle of the tithe as of the Sabbath?

After asserting categorically that the Sabbath law no longer applies to New Testament Christians, a widely used catechism asks: "Why then do we observe Sundays and other Christian festivals?" The answer given is this: "Not by divine command, but that we may have time and opportunity for public divine worship." To preserve God's honor in the tithe principle as we preserve it in the Sabbath principle we should be free to say: "New Testament Christians practice the tithe withholding principle not by divine command but in order that they may worthily honor the Giver and faithfully share with Him the firstfruits of His gifts." This much is certain, and the most discerning theologian cannot contest the point: *We are as fully justified to speak of the Lord's tithe as of the Lord's Day.* To accept the Lord's Day principle without question and to insist that this principle does not apply equally to the Lord's tithe does not have the ring of truth.

In adopting the tithe we have the satisfaction of knowing that we are following the pattern which God Himself laid down for His children in the Old Testament. Moreover, the tithe principle provides a safe guideline to determine a goal toward which to aspire. Another point in favor of tithing is the experience of those who have practiced it. One looks in vain to find a tither who has regretted being one. The writer has met hundreds of people who are supremely happy in giving the tithe to the Lord, but he has never met one person who was sorry that he chose to do so.

Dr. Francis Pieper, a theological giant in the Lutheran Church, expressed this opinion: "One would expect that the New Testament Christian would incline to begin where the Old Testament believer left off." There are some princely givers who have recognized that their standing on the higher ground of grace invites an even higher level of giving than the tithe. One problem may arise in promoting the tithe principle: Someone who is all for it may try to induce another person to adopt it before he is ready to do so. This rule is inviolable: Whatever percentage a person decides to set aside for the Lord must be a step of faith and not of law. If it is to be a step of faith, then it must be done willingly, in sincere conscience, free from any kind of pressure from without.

Many have found the tithe a gateway to the splendid avenue of a large and consecrated ministry of giving, experiencing therein abounding proof of the Lord's blessings. Tithing churches give far more generously to Kingdom causes than nontithing churches. Whether in the career of individual churches or individual Christians, tithing has been tested a thousand times in the laboratory of human experience and has never failed to give proof that it is of God. The person who advocates tithing is the one who practices it; the person who rejects tithing is usually the one who has never tried it. Most tithers enjoy tithing because they have experienced its rewards. *One almost never finds a person giving up tithing after practicing it for any length of time.*

Some Christian men at the head of prosperous business firms assert their belief that tithing the firm's net profit has been the secret of success. They regard this a way of making Christ a member of the board of directors. Though success stories do not always provide a reliable guide, as circumstances vary with each case, it appears that tithing and success often go hand in hand. Mr. Thomas Kane, who openly advances the theory that tithing brings material prosperity, said: "My belief is that God blesses in temporal as well as in spiritual things. The man who honors Him by setting aside a stated portion of his income to His service will in turn be honored by Him. I have never known an exception to this principle."

Charles Page was down to his last dollar when a Salvation Army girl assured him he would prosper if he would tithe. He did better; he gave the girl 15 cents for God's work. Some time later he went to Tulsa, Okla., and struck oil. In an almost fantastic way he found oil almost wherever he drilled. His explanation was: "I think I have missed only two holes in my life. You see, I couldn't miss, for I was in partnership with the Big Fellow and He made geology."

Alvin Dark, all-star shortstop, former manager of the San Francisco Giants and currently of the Cleveland Indians, had this to say: "Giving the first tenth of my income back to God was just as unquestioned in our home as putting on my socks before my shoes. A nickel out of every 50 cents was quite a lot when I got up every day before dawn to peddle my paper route. But as the years went by and my income increased, I found that I could never win in this game of giving to God—He always outgave me. He gave to me physically, financially, and in a dozen other ways. He led me into a satisfying career in baseball. Actually, if I belong to Him, He owns me and my income too, all of it. I have learned that tithing is just a symbol of my trust in Him."

The late R. G. Le Tourneau gave this stirring testimony: "The minute I started my partnership with God, business boomed. The next year my sales were over $100,000; the second year over $150,000; the third year over $200,000. It kept going like that in leaps and bounds until our sales, in 1939, were over $7,000,000, later $40,000,000."

It is not surprising that many believe that tithing brings material prosperity. Many Christians have experienced that faithfulness in giving and prosperity go hand in hand. Nevertheless, no Christian would ever think of tithing as merely a good commercial transaction. Tithing might help a man gain the whole world; but if his reason for tithing is to gain the world, he can be sure that the world is all he will gain. Bargaining with God never has any place in the worship and devotion of a Christian. On the other hand, it is profane to suggest that a sincere Christian who tithes is doing so to trade on God's goodness. It is proper and charitable to assume that the Christian who tithes is doing so in trust, in the confidence that it is God's will for him. Ultimately, all that can be said about tithing and stewardship may be summarized in a simple statement which every Christian can understand and act upon in good faith: *"I will stay true to God's principles; I know He will stay true to His promises."*

Cultivating the Stewardship Life

A minister wanted to spur his congregation to a large response to a special offering for a ministry to mentally retarded people. In his sermon this honest and good man engaged in condemnation of himself, of his congregation, and of society for failing to provide adequately for these afflicted people. Challenging his congregation to follow his example, he suggested that all make a substantial financial pledge for this cause, payable over the next 3 years. To the writer, who was present in that service, the pastor's stance in this case seemed both improper and prejudicial. The charge that very little had been done to help these unfortunate people simply wasn't true. It would have been much more effective had the pastor acknowledged with appreciation that much was indeed being done for them, that a fair percentage of our tax dollars goes for this work, that the church has been engaged in these ministries for years, and that all members by virtue of their regular support of the church's budget have a share in this work. This would have had a much better psychological effect on the congregation. The pastor had a fine opportunity to say that citizens are paying taxes which include causes like this, and that in consideration of such ministries they ought to give their taxes cheerfully, even thankfully, and with a prayer for their most effective use. He could have pointed out that while much was being done, more needed to be done. This would have invited a re-evaluation of the church's Christian work program to determine if a larger part of its entrusted funds ought to be given to such ministries.

It may, in fact, be injudicious to propose any cause, however worthy, as an occasion for a special offering or for increased giving. Obviously, anyone can suggest a dozen causes at any time which may be just as worthy as the one presently under the spotlight. Our giving to God is determined, as we have been saying, not by needs, not by the budget, not by someone's ability to make a cause attractive, but by our decision to be good stewards of God's entrusted gifts. *No needs can match our need to be good stewards.* We are good stewards because God has made His abode in us and His love dwells in us. Nevertheless, because a godly person retains his sinful human nature, he needs the strength and inspiration that comes from knowing that his giving is accomplishing a lot of good. It was this feeling of joy and privilege in giving that led St. Paul to refer to it as "the grace of God that was bestowed upon me" (1 Cor. 15:10). When seen in terms of all the good it does, Christian stewardship is indeed a gift of grace. This idea of stewardship as a noble endowment of grace deserves more prominent attention than it generally receives. The Sunday worship service provides perhaps the best opportunity to restore this idea to its deserving place of honor.

The Sunday Worship Service

There is a two-way action in the divine liturgy: God gives to us, and we give to God. One dimension — God meeting man with His abundant gifts — is *sacramental*

action; the other—man hearing, praising, glorifying God with heart and hand and voice—is *sacrificial* action.

We should expect something really great to happen in the Sunday service. It is an exciting thought that the living Christ is present to impart His gifts to each and every one. But only the questing heart will experience the satisfied need. The expectant soul will receive refreshment from on high. The person who brings to the service a halfhearted, neutral, take-it-or-leave-it attitude will leave it, almost certainly, without any blessing. He expected nothing when he came, and he had nothing when he left. It is, in fact, just because there is so much to receive and so much to give that there is also so much to miss and to ignore. *Church attendance can never be a neutral experience; it always leaves us better or worse.*

We call our public worship assembly a divine service because God serves us and we serve Him. First we accept the gifts God wants us to have; thereupon we offer the gifts God wants us to give. The man who loses the healthy balance between receiving and giving not only misses the joy and purpose of the divine service but may also be in the way of taking the grace of God in vain.

The Sunday service ought to become a weekly high peak of inspiration for every Christian. It is, after all, our highest and holiest exercise this side of heaven and the beginning of an activity which extends into eternity. Here we not only show God's worth to us, but also sense anew our worth to Him and the importance of our position as His agents and ambassadors. Our Sundays around the living Christ will have momentous meaning to the one who sees himself as a working partner with the Lord, sharing the Lord's burden to lift humanity into the new world of grace and joy and peace and hope through the Gospel of redemption. A divine service of worship without any reference to the divine service of ministry and mission performed by the members falls short of its purpose. People cannot be reminded too often that the church is not merely a field upon which a few people are to expend labor, but a force to extend the friendship and love of Christ to the neighborhood and the world. Church members will thank God for His grace in their stewardship when they are led to see their position of honor and dignity in the army of the Lord. *The positive recognition of, and gratitude for, the good ministries of God's children, however inadequate, is always better than a negative denunciation of their failure to do more or to do better.* Sending people home with a sense of failure and defeat is bad psychology and bad theology. They should leave the church with a feeling of gratitude for God's blessings in Christ and the resolve to be inspired by them to worthy discipleship.

The Sunday divine service provides the best opportunity for the nurture of the stewardship life. When stewardship instruction becomes a special campaign, people may begin to regard it as something special in itself, quite apart from daily Christian living. A golden opportunity is missed when any single Sunday service offers nothing to build up the stewardship life of the congregation. Everybody knows that people resent the constant talking about money. All Christians, however, respond joyfully to deeper insights into, and wider outlooks upon, the place and power of stewardship in their lives. Many appeals have a way of getting people down. Stewardship light and inspiration has a way of lifting them up.

The Chief Steward

Being almost exclusively in control of the Sunday service, the pastor is the key man in promoting stewardship understanding. Pastoral stewardship power and congregational stewardship power are vitally linked together. The pastor can preach effectively only what he himself practices faithfully. His own stewardship views and actions will sooner or later be known and followed. Every pastor should follow the example of a doctor of theology who, living with his son, a doctor of medicine, one day received a telephone inquiry, "Is this the doctor who preaches or the one who practices?" to which the pastor answered, "I sincerely hope it is one who does both." One pastor, whose ministry was conspicuously weak, suggested in a ministers' conference that he considered it beneath the dignity of his office to contribute to his own salary. This was another way of saying that he had no desire or intention to be a good steward of God's entrusted gifts. The real tragedy here is that this man not only deprived himself and his family but perhaps hundreds of others of the privilege and blessing that follows faithful stewardship.

Whether he knows it or not, the pastor is in a position of prime responsibility and influence in building up the stewardship life of the church. People may not always get what he says, but they will always get what he is and does. They will know whether his main reason for teaching stewardship is to get the bills of the church paid or to get people into the right relationship with God. His words and actions will prove him a narrow-visioned man who wants patrons to support the church, or a far-visioned man who wants disciples to do Christ's mission among men.

Each Sunday service gives opportunity to emphasize, either before or after the offering is received, another phase of the offering's unique character. In this way God's children will be led to think of their offering as a highly meaningful act. They will be on guard against letting it become a glib tossing of an arbitrary amount of money upon the offering plate wholly unrelated to faith and the amount received from God. It now becomes a joyful affirmation of faith:

Inspired by the Holy Spirit
Following a conscientious decision
Proceeding out of a heart sanctified by faith
Related to Christ's sacrifice
Linked with Christ's power
Dedicated to the advancement of the Kingdom
Sent on its way with prayer
Invested in heavenly treasures

Christian stewards are entitled to the joyful and satisfying feeling that comes to the person who can say: "In my gifts, expressing my faith and love, I am at work in the world. I am lighting candles of hope, singing the song of salvation for the joyless, giving cupfuls of the water of life to the thirsting; I am feeding the hungry, clothing the naked, visiting the sick, and proclaiming the Gospel of liberty and life."

116

The Sunday service folder may be used as an effective agency to strengthen and purify the congregation's stewardship consciousness. To be imbued with enthusiasm for the stewardship life, people must grow up on a regular diet of stewardship vitamins. Growing up on this diet, people will grow into it. Stewardship is as much caught as it is taught. To teach it only in connection with a money-raising effort will debase it and render it impotent. The stewardship theme, the most frequent of all themes on the lips of Jesus, is so vast that it will be adequately presented only by constant repetition. To use the Sunday service folder to inform people that the church is behind or ahead of the needs of the budget, to report the total of last week's offerings, to push the panic button about the dilemma which the church will be in if people don't come through — all this contributes to stewardship weakness and will never produce stewardship power. This sort of thing helps to fix the image of the church as that of an ecclesiastical bill collector.

One church invited its members to suggest stewardship thoughts or sentences to be published in the Sunday folder. There are enough of such Scripture verses to supply a new verse each week for several years. People have ready defenses against mere human appeals, but they will ultimately yield to God's light if indeed they are children of light.

7

God's Power
Backs His Promises

Stewardship Seen as a Mystery

Like the Gospel, stewardship is a mystery. In Biblical language a mystery is a reality so far above human understanding that it would never be known if it had not been revealed by the Holy Spirit. Even after such revelation the mystery cannot be accepted or acted upon without the Spirit's aid.

There is a curious thing about a divine mystery. It is as clear as day to those who accept it in faith, act upon it, and experience its promises, but it remains hidden from others. Jesus thanked the Father for the intimate circle of believers in the mysteries "hidden from the learned and wise but revealed to the simple" (Matt. 11:25 NEB). Simple believers who travel the open road of faith with God in preference to the narrow path of their own reasoning are the blessed and happy ones.

Faith Is the Key

Faith opens the door to the miraculous mysteries of stewardship. Unbelief dismisses the stewardship promises. Faith accepts them. But there is a peculiar quirk in the human mind which plagues even the man of faith. He thinks that God is so spiritual that He has little interest in material things. Thus he finds it easier to accept God's promise, "Believe and be saved" than His promise, "Give and it shall be given to you." Man is a natural-born materialist and "do it yourselfer." Even after his new birth by the Spirit, he harbors the notion that the realm of the spirit is God's domain whereas material things are under his own jurisdiction. But God is not against material values — He gives them. *What offends God is man's hankering for material gifts apart from any interest in Him who is their Source.* Sinful materialism accepts God's gifts and then orders the Giver off the premises. Christian "materialism" honors the Giver even more than His gifts.

The person who trusts God for spiritual but not for material gifts is a half-believer. He presumes to select which of God's promises to believe and which not to believe. Eventually, and inevitably, he will doubt all of them.

How the Mystery Works Out

Stewardship may be thought of as a mystery wrought by the power of God. It is all quite above human understanding. A man simply does not have more by giving more. He doesn't find by losing. Yet that is precisely what the power of God makes possible through the mystery of stewardship. It is as true as God's promises and as possible to experience in the concrete test as God's power to make the promises come true. It is when the man of faith trusts God's promises enough to lean his full weight upon them that he discovers the momentous mystery at work here.

This truth is illustrated by the yarn about the man known in the community for his fondness of children, who had laid a new driveway leading to his garage. When he saw children scribble initials and push handprints into the new cement, the great child-lover stormed out of his house, clenched his fists, scolded the kids, and sent them scrambling in all directions. An amused neighbor chuckled,

"Why, John, I thought you loved children." "I do," John said, "but I love them in the abstract, not in the concrete."

Many accept God's stewardship teachings in an abstract sort of way, with no thought of applying them to the concrete situation of their own lives. But the miracles of the stewardship mystery are never experienced in the abstract. "In keeping of them there is great reward" (Ps. 19:11). This fact confronts us all with a dilemma. We shall have to try it to experience that it is true, and we shall have to believe it to try it. Here experience is the best, though the most challenging, teacher. Actual experience first gives the test, and only then teaches the lesson. Hardheaded stubbornness keeps man from believing, testing, and experiencing the truth of God's promises. There is in each of us a bit of "doubting Thomas." We need the Lord's reminder, "Blessed are they that have not seen and yet have believed" (John 20:29). God's promises are true when given in word even before they are experienced in deed. This is an important lesson for us to learn.

God's Power as We Experienced It

At the beginning of this book we promised an adventure into God's Word to discover a better way of gaining support for Kingdom causes. In subsequent chapters the results of this blest quest were laid down. Now we come face to face with the inevitable question: "Do you have proof positive that God's stewardship way has worked out in the concrete situation?" Though we reject the view that God's promises need proof of their trustworthiness, and though we find the spirit of trumpet-sounding reprehensible, we are thankful that we can present good credentials for our case by reporting our stewardship experiences.

What, then, are the facts about our experiment? Testing the promises in the concrete area of life, we experienced proof that:

Good stewardship instruction produces good stewards.
Pure stewardship truth cuts its own channel into human lives.
A person or a congregation may bank on God's promises without risk.
God's power backs His promises.

As evidence of God's power at work in the stewardship mystery, we certify to our experience in the stewardship of giving and of serving.

Our scale of giving jumped from an annual average of $16 per communicant during the 17 years before our stewardship program began to an average of $44 per active member in 1944 (the year the new program was initiated), to $140 in 1956, to $190 in 1965, and to more than $200 in the subsequent years. To head off any wrong conclusions, two explanations are in order: (1) On the average we were below the lower middle class income level for most of the years from 1944 on, due to radical shifts in the community. (2) The above figures have not been adjusted to scale showing national economic levels and changes in dollar value.

None of us doubted that God had wrought a miracle before our eyes. Few of us had dared to hope for such a shower of abundance. We were now in a position to uphold an ambitious program in local and world evangelism. There was no longer any need for the church to manipulate the people's giving. It was the people themselves, constantly matching the Giver's gifts with a faithful stewardship over them, that now gave direction to the church's program of ministry and mission. With this kind of solid financial support, the congregation was enabled to build a new sanctuary and school with auxiliary structures at a cost of about half a million dollars, and to do so without a special campaign for funds, either before or after the construction of the buildings. Each year we placed about $35,000 into the budget for payment on the church debt. Our payments on the debt were as constant as the gifts of God's people, and these in turn were as constant as the gifts of the Giver. It all worked out precisely as God said it would.

There was another distinctive blessing, one that far exceeded the financial element in long-range importance. Through their stewardship convictions our people brought a new mood and spirit of Christian ministry into the congregation. The people were growing in the joy of giving and serving. This is an important point, for in the eyes of God people have not begun to give or serve until they feel glad because of it. When people become imbued with the stewardship spirit, they grow zealous in the desire to serve God and man. This was conspicuously demonstrated in increased church attendance and in enlarged ministries of Christian service. There was always an adequate supply of willing workers for every task. Sometimes it was even difficult to provide enough work for all the people who volunteered for Christian service. The writer does not recall a single instance when a request for some kind of Christian mission was turned down either by the church as such or by individual members.

The character of interest and enthusiasm was notably shifted to ministries that were vitally related to the church's essential mission under Christ. The "moneymaking" and time-wasting activities gave way to the kind of ministries that offer rich compensation to those engaging in them. Members became more and more involved in the things of the Spirit, the vital activities that build life from the inside out. Almost every home in the church was a Covenant Home, pledged to daily Bible reading and prayer; most members accepted the invitation to take the "Journey Through the Bible"; people were laying upon the altar of their love for God the offering of their treasures, their time, and their talents. A program for women's activities was developed that gave each member an opportunity to express her unique talents in some phase of Christ's mission. Children, who usually respond to God's service as readily as flowers open to the sun, joined in the various congregational programs of ministry; the youth groups, proverbially irritated with all sham and phoneyness in the church, responded appreciatively to the good sense and honesty of the stewardship concept of life and supported it loyally.

This beautiful picture is reminiscent of a lovely story whose charm so engaged the interest of three Gospel writers that they included it in their accounts of the life of Jesus (Matt. 26:6-13; Mark 14:3-9; John 12:1-8). The story tells of a delightful act of stewardship on the part of Mary, sister of Martha and Lazarus. It happened at a dinner in Bethany, at the house of Simon the leper, whom Jesus had presumably cured of his disease. Mary, sensing the nearness of the cross, wanted to do something to show her faith and love and to bring comfort to the heart of Jesus, heavy with foreboding about the events ahead. What she did became a living sermon and memorial to the end of time, as Jesus said it would.

"Mary took a pound of ointment of spikenard, very costly, and anointed the feet of Jesus, and wiped His feet with her hair, and the house was filled with the odour of the ointment." (John 12:3)

The atmosphere grew tense from the taunts of the disciples. The insolent Judas, resenting the lost opportunity to grab a share of Mary's gift for himself, impugned the integrity both of Mary and, indirectly, of Jesus: "Why was not this ointment sold . . . and given to the poor?" (John 12:5). Jesus' response gave the disciples of that day and of ours much to ponder: "Let her alone," He said. "She has done a beautiful thing to Me. . . . She has anointed My body beforehand for burying. . . . Wherever the Gospel is preached in the whole world, what she has done will be told in memory of her." (Mark 14:6-9 RSV)

Taking the single strands of Mary's stewardship act, Jesus wove them together and fashioned them into a precious diadem to crown her head through all eternity.

Mary's act was beautiful because of the faith behind it. "She has anointed My body beforehand for burying," Jesus said. Sitting at Jesus' feet and hearing His words, Mary had learned all about God's love, the cross, the grave, the crown. She both believed and loved.

Mary's act was beautiful because of its timeliness. "I will beat death to Him," she said, and she did. Sometimes we wait too long, and our gifts of love arrive too late.

Mary's act was beautiful because of its generosity. She didn't count the cost. She didn't think of it as loss to herself. She knew that nothing could be counted as loss if it expressed love and pleased Christ.

Mary's act was beautiful because of the example it left. The fragrance of that costly ointment filled the room, and it has never stopped filling human hearts and homes.

Jesus said, "Wherever the Gospel is preached in the whole world, what she has done will be told in memory of her." At this very moment we are showing the truth of Jesus' prophecy. After us others will be doing the same thing. To the end of time and beyond it, Mary's beautiful act stands as a memorial of her faith and love.

Our acts of faith and love are likewise precious to the Savior and bring Him joy. In His eyes they too are a beautiful work, an abiding memorial.